Conquer Your Emotions

First Printed in Great Britain by
Obex Publishing Ltd in 2020

2 4 6 8 10 9 7 5 3 1

Paperback ISBN   978-1-913454-07-4
eBook ISBN   978-1-913454-08-1

A CIP catalogue record for this book is available
from the British Library.

Obex Publishing Ltd.
Reg. No. 12169917

CONTENTS

Introduction

Do you consider yourself to be an emotional kind of person?

Do you find yourself relatively small and insignificant problems badly?
Are you easily affected whenever your emotions change from one side of the spectrum to the other?
Are you someone who only has to be within a few feet of a Disney film to feel themselves tearing up?

Never fear, you're actually in good company!

Emotions are all-powerful. They have the capacity to take you over the edge, to derail your day completely, and to lead you into situations that you live to regret.

Of course, on the flip-side emotions allow us to feel great joy, happiness, and contentment. The problem is, we don't tend to focus on the positives, and instead, we allow those pesky negative emotions to take a hold of the reins and lead us into situations that aren't where we really want to be.

If you're reading this and nodding your head, this book is for you.

When you allow your emotions to dictate your life and your actions, you have no control. You've completely submitted to the whim of your emotions and as a result, anything can happen. One minute you're happy, the next you're sad; one minute you're productive and getting through your daily to-do list, and the next you're unable to focus, and you're crying in a toilet.

This is a far more common situation than you can understand right now, but that doesn't mean it's an acceptable one.

Learning how to take back control of your emotions and steer them where you want them to go is possible. It takes time and effort, but it's entirely possible. Once you've conquered your emotions, once you're the one with the reins in your hand, you can steer your day where you want it to go.

Sure, you're still going to feel; why would you want to avoid that? It's part of life! You're going to feel positive emotions, and you're still going to feel negative ones, but the difference is that they won't completely take you over as they did before. You can experience them, allow them to teach you what they need to, and you can overcome them.

You are more powerful than you know. You are more in control than you realise right now.

All you need to do is learn, open your mind, and focus on personal growth.

So, if you're reading this and nodding along, your journey starts here. If you're reading it and shaking your head, considering it to be another chunk of mumbo jumbo, then give it a chance. Just read through and see how you feel at the end. The chances are you'll start to think there's something in it, try a few exercises we're going to go through, and boom! Emotional control is yours.

The only person who needs to control how you feel and what you do as a result of those feelings is you.

So, make yourself comfortable, take a deep breath, and prepare to conquer the maelstrom of emotions whirling around inside you.

Chapter 1:

Your One-Stop Guide to Emotions

What are emotions?

You can't see them, you can't hear them or smell them, but you can certainly feel them.

As humans, we tend to give more credibility to the things we can see, because they feel safe to us. When we can see something, we think we're able to control it. We can catch it, measure it, study it, and understand it. When we can't see it, that's when we become a little worried.

Yes, we humans are control freaks.

We like to understand and study, and emotions elude us completely in that way.

The problem is, by not giving enough credibility and understanding to how emotions are formed and what they can do if you allow them to run riot, you're effectively allowing them to run the show.

This book is about learning to control your emotions and steering them where you want them to go, learning now to be at the whim of a passing yet strong emotion, and using them for the greater good. However, before you get to that point, you need some background information. It's not possible to be able to control something you don't understand.

With that in mind, this chapter is going to talk about what emotions actually are, where they come from, what causes them, how they're formed, and the control they can have over you. By the end, you're not going to be a psychologist by any means, but you'll understand the basics of emotional formation and where on Earth these pesky feelings actually come from in the first place. Let's get started.

What Are Emotions?

Whether you call them emotions or feelings, they're one and the same.

Basically, you're human because you have the capacity to feel. You're capable of feeling happiness and joy, but you're also capable of feeling hate, greed, panic, and fear. There are both negative and positive emotions, but we are often taken away by the negative ones because they are connected to fear. When we fear something, our psychological response is much stronger.

However, we'll talk about that a little later on.

For now, you need to know that there is a difference between an emotion and a mood. An emotion is something you feel, a reaction to an event or a situation. Emotions pass quite quickly, although they can be intense.

On the other hand, a mood can last a little while longer. Emotions can cause a mood, and they can be experienced within a mood, but they're not one and the same.

We mentioned earlier that humans worry about emotions because they can't be seen and measured, and scientists are in the same boat. The problem comes down to the fact that everyone feels something slightly differently, or to a different degree. You might feel happiness completely differently to the way your friend feels it. You might experience love in a totally different way to your partner. It doesn't mean one emotion is more valid than the other, it's simply the fact that we all experience feelings in a way that is personal to us.

We're all individual, after all.

You will come across people who feel things more strongly than others, and you'll come across those who are able to handle the way they feel and put it to the back of their minds. The problem is, there is no magical 'off' switch for emotions. You can't turn them off when they become a little too troublesome. What you can do is learn how to handle them, turn them into something useful and avoid them derailing your day.

In order for an emotion to be formed, you need three components:

• Subjective emotion
• A physical response to that emotion
• An expressive component of that emotion

That sounds as clear as mud at this point, so let's explore each one a little more deeply, to help you understand what emotions are and how they're formed.

Subjective Emotion

You cannot measure a subjective emotion because it's completely personal. A subjective emotion is all about how you define it and how you express it. For instance, one person in a relationship might feel that they need hearts and flowers, gifts and huge gestures of romance in order to feel loved. The other person might feel that simply spending time together and having experiences is enough. That doesn't mean they don't love each other the same, or that one loves the other less, it's simply that they experience the subjective emotion differently. It's about perspective, and it's unique to you.

Scientists had subjective emotions because they can't be measured. They have no clue how to even begin, and it's not likely to be developed any time soon!

A Physical Response to That Emotion

The physical response can be measured and evaluated because it can be seen. This is the action as a result of the subjective emotion. So, you might blush when you're embarrassed, you might cry when you're sad and you might laugh when you feel awkward. These are physical responses to your emotions. A few others associated with common emotions are:

- A thumping heartbeat
- Shaking
- Sweating
- Becoming teary
- Stumbling over your words
- Falling over or suddenly becoming clumsy
- An inability to concentrate or feeling distracted
- Blushing

You can see these responses, which tell the person standing next to you that you're experiencing a specific emotion. What they don't know is what the emotion is. For instance, you might blush when you're around someone you feel attracted to, but you might also blush when you're embarrassed or caught out. Only you know what you're feeling, but the cues you're showing to the outside world give a few suggestions.

These physical responses come from something called the 'fight or flight' response. Basically, when your mind experiences something it considers to be a threat, it releases hormones to help your body deal with it, to either fight it or run away from it. The problem is, your brain isn't always accurate with what it considers a threat, so you might experience the stress response when there's nothing to be afraid of.

Aside from that, these physical responses are your body's way of keeping you safe, even if there is nothing to be kept safe from in the first place!

An Expressive Component to That Emotion

Expressive reactions are very similar to physical ones, and they can't really be controlled. You can learn how to control the emotion by recognising it and calming yourself down at the moment, but the way your body reacts to it cannot be changed if it is allowed to raise up and take control.

Expressive components are linked to body language. Of course, body language speaks volumes when words don't! You can show that you're nervous without actually saying a word because your body is screaming "I'm really scared right now!" In a job interview, you might be displaying nervous body language without even knowing about it. Expressive components give a clue to anyone in the vicinity about how you're feeling, and you might not even be aware you're doing it.

A few expressive components include:

- A hesitation or a pause
- A quick intake of breath, i.e. shock
- A raised eyebrow
- Tearing up and crying
- Freezing for a second
- Tensing your muscles

- Changing the way you speak, e.g. tone of voice suddenly goes up or down
- Displaying defensive body language, e.g. crossing arms or legs over your body

It's easy to recognise these reactions in other people, and as a result, you'll learn to read others far more easily. This is great for improving your interpersonal skills.

Why Do We Even Have Emotions?

We know we have emotions because we're human, but why?

We feel different emotions because that's what we're supposed to do. That is all that scientists and researchers can actually learn to agree on where this subject is concerned. However, we also know that we don't feel things the same as one another, and that's what makes us unique.

One theory which many researchers generally agree on is that emotions link back to that fight or flight response we mentioned earlier. Emotions help to keep you safe because they highlight a situation that could be a problem, a threat, or something which could turn out to be hurtful. For example, if you experience a situation that makes you freeze for a second, that's your body telling you that something could be dangerous and makes you feel fear. That emotion then helps you decide what action to take in order to avoid the problem.

The bottom line is that we can't give you a solid reason as to why we feel emotions because researchers and scientists haven't figured it out themselves yet. There are countless theories flying around - some believe we're born with a full set of emotions, other feelings we develop them over time, whilst others believe that triggers bring previously unknown emotions to the fore. Perhaps this is what makes being human so wonderful - there are countless things we still don't understand!

Our emotions are what make us unique, so perhaps that's a good enough argument for why we should be embracing them and learning how to control them, rather than pushing them away and trying not to experience them at all!

At the end of the day, feeling something is better than feeling nothing at all.

Why Do Some People 'Feel' Things More Keenly Than Others?

This is an interesting question to explore a little.

Why do some people tend to 'feel' things more strongly than other people? For instance, you've probably met someone who is more sensitive than other people you know; perhaps that's you. When something happens, they feel like they're being taken over by their sadness or their anger, whilst others can feel it but only slightly.

Nobody really knows why this is the case, however, shortly we're going to talk about a part of the brain called the amygdala. It is thought that those who feel things more strongly, perhaps those who consider themselves to be an empath, have a highly functioning or more sensitive amygdala.

Of course, it could actually be that those who feel things aren't so highly experienced in terms of how to control their emotions, whilst those who feel it but aren't taken over by it have. That's just one theory that could explain it, but again, we have no solid explanation!

The Role of the Amygdala

If you read about the brain, you'll no doubt hear about the amygdala.

The amygdala is a small part of the brain, part of the limbic system, and its main role is memory processing and emotional processing. Put simply, emotions aren't necessarily stored in the amygdala, but they spend a lot of time being processed and recognised there, which is why most people will link this part of the brain with emotional storage and recognition. It is the amygdala that also plays a part in the fight or flight stress response, so you can tell from that explanation that the amygdala is quite high prevalent with negative emotional responses too.

You could say that the amygdala is a processing centre and it receives messages from our main senses and all the main organs within our bodies. It then takes this information, decades it and interprets it. It also works closely with the hippocampus, which is usually related to memory storage and recognition. When an emotion is felt, the information linked to that emotion, e.g. a past experience, is pulled to the front of your mind, to help you decide what to do about it, e.g. fight it, face it, or run away from it.

Put simply, the memories of the emotion are in the hippocampus, and the actual emotion itself is in the amygdala. These two parts of the brain then work together to manifest the emotional response you feel.

Points to Remember
From This Chapter

We've covered a lot of ground in this chapter, but despite all the theories and the explanations, we still don't have a solid reason for what an emotion is and why we have it. Scientists haven't figured it out yet and quite frankly, they probably never will!

What we can agree on is that we feel because we're human and that how we feel and to what degree we feel, make us unique.

The main points to take from this chapter are:

- Emotions are the same as feelings
- We feel emotions because we're human, but they cannot be seen or measured effectively
- Scientists have long tried to study emotions and come to a solid idea of why we experience them but are yet to come up with anything conclusive
- Emotions are however thought to be tied to the stress response, i.e. 'fight or flight' and are designed to help us recognise threats and keep us safe
- You need a subjective emotion, a physiological response, and an expressive component in order to experience a full emotion
- Some people feel emotions more strongly than others, and whilst that could be down to the

sensitivity of the amygdala, it could also be down to emotional control techniques learnt over a lifetime

- The amygdala is a part of the brain which is connected to memories and emotions.

Chapter 2:

What Happens When You Let Your Emotions Have All the Control?

Emotions are designed to be useful, but that doesn't mean that they are all the time.

When you allow your emotions to control you, you're actually allowing them to dictate your actions and could cause you to act in a way that you may regret later.

The whole point of this book is to help you learn how to control your emotions and conquer them, so they don't force you into situations that could become harmful to you or the relationships in your life. That doesn't mean you don't feel them, or you try and push them down, but it means you allow yourself to recognise the emotion and learn when something is affecting you in a negative way.

We're going to cover many techniques later in the book which allows you to harness the power of your emotions and use them for good, rather than allowing them to derail your good intentions. For now, we need to explore the other side of the coin, i.e. what happens when you allow negative emotions to get the better of you.

Consider this chapter a cautionary tale. This is the other side of the story - what may happen if you continue to go down the same route. By the end of this chapter, you should be very clear in your mind that the only route to go down is then, which allows you control over your emotions and not the other way around.

So, let's look at what not being the one in control can actually do.

Emotions Can Affect Your Productivity Levels

Have you ever started the day in a perfectly good state of mind? You have good intentions; you're going to go to work, and you're going to work through your to-do list. You're pretty sure that today is the day you're going to actually achieve that feat.

It's all going well until you head off on your scheduled break and you start scrolling through your social media feeds to pass the time. You then see a picture that you wish you hadn't seen. Perhaps it is a picture of an ex who is happy with someone else. Maybe it's a piece of news that you didn't want to read about or something which triggers you back to a time which caused you distress.

How do you feel at that moment?

Sad? Angry? Jealous?

Are you able to push that emotion aside at the end of your coffee break and go back to your desk, returning to the hopeful state of mind you were in before?

Not likely.

It's more likely that you'll focus on the thing you've seen the emotion that is rising up as a result of it.

Your heart might race, you might sweat, you might have tears in your eyes, and you might begin to blush. These are all effects of an emotion that is threatening to overtake your day. Your focus levels might go out of the window, and instead of being focused on ticking items off your to-do list, you're still thinking about the picture or piece of news you've just seen.

For some, this is fleeting. The general idea is that emotions last for 90 seconds before they begin to dissipate, but the emotional reaction could last considerably longer.

So, by the time you've finished raging and letting the day get away from you, the emotion has passed, but the reaction to it hasn't. You've now missed deadlines, you're not as productive as you were at the start of the day, and several items remain unticked on your to-do list.

For many, this is a common situation. When a problem occurs, they're not able to overcome it and focus, instead, they allow it to derail the day completely, and it ends up being a complete non-starter. It's normally the case that by the end of the day when everything has settled down, you begin to rue the lost hours you missed focusing on something which really wasn't worth it.

You see, you can't take the time back.

When Your Anger Gets
The Better of You

Another very common situation which arises from allowing emotions to control you is when you encounter anger.

We're all more than capable of experience anger. Some people are generally a little angrier than others, whilst some people are able to deal with their anger in more useful ways, e.g. via exercise. However, anger is a regular and normal human emotion that we all feel at some stage in our lives.

You'll no doubt have heard the adage of "seeing red". When you're angry, you literally can't think or see straight, but anger is a very fast-passing emotion. By the time you've overcome the original anger, you might have acted out in a way that will take a lot longer to fix.

For instance, perhaps you become angry at something your friend told you. You allow your anger to rise up and overtake you, and as a result, you say something which you can't take back. Once those words are out of your mouth, that's it. The game's over.

Your friend may forgive you, but who's to say they will?

Anger can make you say and do things which you spend days, weeks, or even months trying to put right. All because of an emotion that lasted no more than a couple of minutes at most. Anger is probably the most damaging of all human emotions, perhaps jealousy aside.

We do things when we're angry, and we look back at them in astonishment afterwards. We might be shocked that we are capable of saying or doing such things, and we might feel terribly guilty as a result of it. As you can see, one emotion can sometimes lead to another - anger often leads to guilt or shame.

Being able to harness anger isn't easy, but it's something which can be learnt. As a result, you can avoid these situations occurring, and you can use that raw power for good, allowing it to become a motivator towards success, rather than a situation you wish that you weren't in the middle of.

Situations You May Regret

It's not just anger which can cause you to end up in a bad situation, and we've already mentioned jealousy as another one. Even positive emotions can actually cause you to think in a one-sided manner, and you might end up saying something insensitive to someone going through a hard time, who will then take offence.

As you can see, emotions, in general, can cause you to get into situations that you look back on and regret. The reason they do is this because they overtake your thinking for just a second, and in that second you can easily say or do something you wouldn't have done otherwise.

For instance, let's think about a work situation.

What if you're sat around a meeting room table, and you're trying to come up with ideas. You have a great idea, and for a second you're filled with joy and pride because everyone complimented you on your idea. Then, someone else tries to add something to your idea, and you accidentally say something demeaning to them, because you were so caught up in the moment of joy you were experiencing.

They're going to be upset, they're going to be offended, and they might even be angry because they take what you said as disrespect.

It's vital to understand that emotions can put you into situations that are hard to manage. However, by being the one in control, you're able to recognise these situations and avoid disaster as a result.
That is what this book aims to teach you how to do.

Points to Remember
From This Chapter

This chapter has been an informational one. It is designed to show you what could happen if you don't maintain control over your feelings. It's very easy for your emotions to put you into situations that cause you severe harm in the future. Sure, they might be fleeting little problems, but do you want to be in that situation at all?

The main points to take from this chapter are:

- Emotions have the power to take over your actions and your words for a split second; during that time, the damage could already be done
- It's possible for positive emotions to lead you into situations too if you're not able to handle yourself at the moment
- Negative emotions tend to lead onto other negative emotions, e.g. anger often leads to guilt or shame
- Learning how to control your emotions will enable you to still feel what you're supposed to feel, but give you a better chance at side-stepping any potentially damaging outcomes.

Chapter 3:
The Power of The Ego

Now we know what emotions are and how they're formed, we can delve a little deeper. The first thing we come into contact with is the ego.

You're no doubt aware of the ego, it's something we use in a derogative term whenever we meet someone we feel is over-arrogant or someone who has an inflated sense of self-importance. We say something "oh they've got such an ego" or use the word 'egotistical'.

The thing is, we all have an ego, whether we want to believe it or not.

Understanding what the ego is and learning how it can actually control your emotions and force you to act in a certain way is vital if you want to ascertain any amount of control of your own emotions and keep them within your grasp on the reins.

What is The Ego?

The ego is, to make it as simple as possible, what you believe of yourself to be. It's your self-image, the way you see yourself and what you project onto yourself. Your ego can be positive, negative, or a mixture of the two.

Very confident people may have a label as being arrogant or egotistical, but it's simply that their ego tells them they're the best at what they do, they can overcome anything, etc. There are of course good sides to being confident and bad sides, and it depends on which side of the spectrum you fall!

You're not born with your ego, it's something which develops over time. As you have life experiences, your view of yourself shifts and changes, and that helps to develop your ego into the place it's at now. The problem is, when you allow your ego to get a little out of control, it can start to affect your behaviour and your action, based on what your emotions are.

You can't see the ego, it's not something you can measure or visualise, it's simply a state of mind. Your ego often hides behind what you believe to be true, but your opinions and thoughts may not be the truth at all. Put simply, your ego has a very firm attachment to your own identity, and as a result, it can be quite short-sighted and limiting.

Why is The Ego so Damaging?

The reason the ego has such a negative connotation is that it links to negative emotions and situations far more than it does positive. When positive things come our way, we tend to just accept them, celebrate it a little and let it go. However, when negative things come our way, we tend to dwell on them a little more, and our reactions and behaviours as a result of them can be more extreme.

You can easily see your ego at work, or the ego of someone else, if you look for emotional reactions. For instance, when someone is experiencing anger, or they're feeling a little insecure, they're feeling that way because of what their ego is telling them. The ego is whispering in their ear, a little like the devil on the shoulder. It's saying "you're not good enough, you're not doing that right, why would they listen to you?" etc.

As a result, the person experiencing the emotion tends to act out. You'll remember in our last chapter we talked about situations you live to regret because of your emotional outburst, and whilst the ego isn't responsible for emotions, it does fire them up and cause them to be more pronounced than they would otherwise be.

Taking the anger situation again. If someone acts out from anger, perhaps says or does something afterwards, the ego might then cause them to feel guilty afterwards, berating itself for what it's done. So, it's not your mind that's in control at this point, it's your ego.

This can be damaging because it eats away at your self-esteem and causes you to act in ways you wish you hadn't. Without having much experience of your own ego, perhaps being unaware of it, it's hard to tell the difference between your ego talking and your own self. This can cause you to become self-critical, and when that happens, your confidence can easily hit the floor.

It's not easy to be upbeat and positive when your own mind is telling you that you're not good enough and berating you for saying or doing something when you were in a state of anger.

Is Ego Always Negative?

We tend to think that the ego is just arrogant, but that's not necessarily the case. Sometimes the ego can simply be very insecure.

When you label someone as having an ego, it generally means that they think they're better than the others around them, but it's possible that their ego is actually lacking in confidence and they're feeling negative in the inside. Again, you can't see the ego, so it's hard to really pinpoint it.

How does this all tie into emotions?

Because whilst your ego doesn't form or control your emotions, it exacerbates them. This isn't necessarily always bad, but more often than not when the ego is in play, the outcome is quite negative in some way.

The bad news? Whilst it's possible to learn how to control your emotions, it's not possible to get rid of your ego. Sorry.

What you can do is learn to harness the power of your emotions and recognise your outbursts and the way you react. By being more mindful, you're actually dumbing your ego down a little, and reducing the negativity it causes.

Points to Remember
From This Chapter

This has been a relatively quick chapter, but an important one nonetheless.

The ego has a part to play in the way in which we allow our emotions to cloud our judgement, causing us to act out in ways which we may later come to regret.

The main points to remember from this chapter are:

- Everyone has an ego
- The ego is something which can't be seen or felt, but it can be shown in the way in which we allow ourselves to be controlled by our emotions and the outburst which follows
- The ego is fragile, meaning it is generally arrogant or lacking in confidence
- The ego doesn't cause emotions, but it does fire up your initial reaction to that emotion
- You cannot learn to control your ego, but by learning to control your emotions, you're able to dumb down your ego, and it will cause less trouble as a result.

Chapter 4:
What Are Emotional Triggers?

If you want to learn how to control your emotions, you need to understand what causes them.

We all have emotions that are attached to certain things, be it a memory, a past experience, a fear, or a belief. When we experience that, our emotions rise as a result. These are known as emotional triggers.

The first step in controlling your own emotions is identifying your personal triggers and working to reduce them as much as possible. However, when you do that, you need to ensure that you're focusing on the right areas, i.e. the trigger which has the most control over you.

Everyone has general triggers, i.e. everyone becomes upset when they see sad news on the TV, and everyone feels happy when they do a good deed. These aren't triggers per se, they're just emotional reactions to general stimuli or events. However, if you feel strongly about a certain thing, an event or anything else, that is a trigger for you. It may not be a trigger for your friend, your sibling, your parents, or anyone else you know, but it is a personal trigger to you.

Emotional Triggers Are Personal to The Individual

The first step in understanding emotional triggers is to know that they're completely individual to the person involved.

We've just mentioned that something which triggers a strong emotion in you may not even affect someone close to you, and that's because the thing which is affecting you, simply isn't a trigger for them. In this case, it's likely to be connected to a personal experience you've had, a memory, or a fear.

A little later we're going to talk about how you can try and reduce the effect of triggers in your life, but it's likely always to be a slight issue for you to some degree. If something affects you very deeply now, you can try your best to overcome it and reduce the effect, but it is likely to still bring a slight reaction in you in the future. How you deal with that trigger however is the thing which can change, and that's what we're aiming towards.

For you, a trigger is something that triggers a flashback or a quick memory in your mind, and it takes you back to that moment when you experienced it, or the deep-rooted fear which is connected to your trigger. It's likely that triggers are more negative than positive, however, and these are the ones you obviously need to try and target.

Common Emotional Triggers

It's impossible to give you a list of triggers because they're so personal to everyone who has them, but we can give you a few examples. As a result, you can look into whether or not these might be triggers of your own.

A few suggestions include:

- Encountering an ex unexpectedly
- Reading news on social media about an ex or someone you care about
- Having to work closely with someone you do not like
- A partner suddenly starts acting a little quiet, and you've been cheated on before, so you assume it's happening again
- A friend cancels one meeting, and you worry they're moving away from you
- Illness or symptoms related to an illness

These are just a few potential triggers so you can see the sorts of things we're talking about. Let's explore them in a bit more detail and explain why they're triggers.

You will, however, notice that they're all negative situations. Remember, we don't really have to do much about positive emotions, it's the negative ones which cause all the problems!

Encountering an ex unexpectedly, perhaps in the street or at a party with mutual friends may trigger memories from the past. If your relationship ended badly, or you didn't want it to end, this is going to quickly run a movie reel through your mind at a fast speed, relaying all the negative things which happened before your union ended. You might feel angry, sad, jealous, betrayed, or you may simply feel a terrible sense of loss.

The same may be said for seeing news about your ex on social media, or someone who you actually have an attraction to. These are all triggers for negative emotions that are related to love and loss.

In these situations, it's very easy for your emotions to get the better of you because anything related to relationships is so emotionally charged. You might feel tears in your eyes and run away, you might say something out of anger which you wish you hadn't, or you might blush and shake, not able to speak at that time.

In this case, seeing your ex is your emotional trigger. How do you get over it? With time, basically. In this case, it's really a matter of allowing yourself to heal and getting closure on the relationship. This person may also have some effect on you, but how you choose to react to it can change over time, as you become more able to control your emotional reactions.

So, how about having to work closely with someone you don't really like too much? This is an emotional trigger because it may bring up emotions such as competitiveness, severe dislike, anxiety, and anger. Depending upon what actually happened to make you dislike this person, depends on the actual emotion you're going to feel, but it's likely to be a very tense situation regardless.

Most of us have one person in our lives who is a real emotional trigger to us. This can be an ex-lover, an ex-friend, someone you simply don't like, or someone who has done you wrong in the past. Whatever they've done, the simple sight of them makes you want to scream, and in that case, they're a personal trigger to you.

The only way to overcome this is to make peace with the person within your own mind. Forgive them, forgive yourself and move on. They might always make your blood boil a little, but your reactions to them will be less visible and less damaging as a result of your new emotional control.

That brings us onto a very common trigger, one which is related to fear.

If you've been cheated on in a relationship in the past, the chances are that the worry and fear of it happening again will be a real emotional trigger for you, for some time afterwards. This might always be a trigger, simply because the memory of the first time it happened is so clearly stamped in your mind.

If a current partner starts to act in a way that is reminiscent of what happened the first time, e.g. they might be a little quiet, they might not answer their phone straight away, then you're going to automatically jump to a conclusion which may not be correct. You'll do this because your emotional trigger is the fear of being cheated on again.

Anger and fear are two of the most damaging emotions because they drive our actions very intensely. Fear is likely to make you jump into action, the fight or flight response will kick in, and as a result, you'll try and overcome a situation that might not even be there.

You might say something to your partner, and they might take serious offence at being accused of cheating when they're not. You might try and do some detective work, tying yourself up in knots and causing yourself severe distress for nothing.

The same kind of situation occurs when a friend cancels on you perhaps once, and you start to think that they've found a better friend to hang out with.

You worry that you're not good enough, perhaps because it's happened before. Again, the same thing goes for anything related to illness. This is another fear-driven emotional response, it's driven by a potential fear of loss, or a fear of being ill, perhaps because of a past experience.

Boosting your self-confidence and learning to see things as they are, relying upon facts rather than assumptions will help you to manage your fears in this way, and as a result, your trigger will become less powerful over time.

There are countless different examples of potential emotional triggers we could give, but every single one of them is driven by an event or a fear which happened before, forcing you to do your best to defend against it. Your amygdala is sparking up at this point, your stress response is intact, and you're doing your best to kick a potential threat from your life.

The problem is, there usually isn't a real fear there at all.

How Can You Identify
Your Own Triggers?

A little later in the book, we're going to talk about something called journalling. This is a great way to try and identify your own emotional triggers, but you can also think about brainstorming too.

Think back over the last few weeks or months, and try and remember the last time you had a particularly strong emotional reaction. Can you remember what happened before it? How did it feel? By trying to pinpoint the events and the way it presented itself to you, you can try and identify whether this is a trigger that you repeatedly deal with or a one-time event.

If you're going to give journaling a try, you'll learn more about this in a later chapter which we're going to dedicate to it. However, for now, you simply need to know that journaling your emotions gives you interesting information to look back over, where you can identify patterns and triggers quite easily.

Once you have an idea of what a few of your potential triggers are, it's best to tackle them one at a time. Most of us have more than one, and it's not a good idea to overload yourself and try and tackle several at the same time. Start with the one which has the most control over you and then work down from there.

You could also ask someone you are close to if they can come up with any specific triggers they have noticed for you. Maybe they can see a pattern emerging that you can't, and this information will prove invaluable. However, make sure you choose someone who knows you well and who is going to be open and honest with you completely.

How to Reduce Your Emotional Triggers

Once you've identified your triggers, how can you try and reduce their impact on your life?

Remember, you may always have the trigger to some degree, but the way you react to it will change as you become more able to control your emotions yourself.

Face The Trigger Head-on

You've no doubt heard the saying "feel the fear and do it anyway", and this is exactly what you're going to do with this suggestion. Yes, it's scary, but sometimes the only way to overcome something, usually a fear, is to go into it, experience it, feel it, and see what happens. 99% of the time you'll see that the worst-case scenario you'd been terrified of doesn't actually even come close to occurring.

After you've faced a trigger once, the second time you encounter it you'll probably still feel the same emotions bubbling up, but perhaps they won't be as strong. The third time you encounter it, you'll be able to take a second to assess what's going on, remember that you've been here before and survived, and as a result, the trigger doesn't hold the same strength or control over you.

Facing an emotional trigger in this way is exactly the same as facing a fear head-on. That makes sense because many emotional triggers are actually fears which we hold deep within, often due to personal and past experiences, or things which have happened to those close to us.

Challenge Yourself
And Question The Trigger

Another strategy is to challenge the trigger and question it intensely. Of course, you need to have identified the trigger as one of your own before you can do this, but once that step is completed, you can unpick it and analyse the control it has over you.

Write the trigger down on a piece of paper and then brainstorm reasons around it as to why it affects you. Is it because you're scared of a situation repeating itself? Are you scared of rejection? Do you worry that harm is going to come to you or someone you're close to? Do you feel embarrassed and you don't like the way it feels? Be honest and write it down; it doesn't matter whether it seems totally ridiculous or not - your emotions are your own, whether they make sense at the moment or not.

Once you've come up with a few reasons as to why this is a trigger for you, address each one. Ask yourself 'what is the worst thing that can happen here?' It's very likely that the worst thing that can happen is something not at all terrible and something you can more than survive.

Challenge your reasons, unpick them and analyse them, ask yourself whether this really matters in the grand scheme of things, right down to the point where the trigger seems quite inconsequential for a second.

When you face that trigger again in the future, quickly pull your brainstorming session to the front of your mind and see whether you're able to feel more in control as a result.

Reduce Your Exposure to The Trigger

This particular method isn't the best one in terms of dealing with something for the long term, but it might help you in the short term.

If you're able to cut yourself off from the trigger and not experience it, go for it. However, you're not actually dealing with the deep issue by doing this. What reducing your exposure could do is allow you the time to work on yourself and your other emotional triggers, before facing this one.

In addition, it's possible that the trigger will lose its power the longer you're not exposed to it. So, if you can limit your exposure or completely avoid it, the next time it does become a problem, you may find that it doesn't bother you in the slightest! Of course, by that time you'll also have learnt how to control your general emotions in a far more effective way, which will give you an advantage.

Overcome the Trigger
by Letting the Past Go

One of the healthiest ways to overcome an emotional trigger is to actually overcome it and let it go. This is easier said than done, for sure, but it's possible with time.

In order to do this, you need to strongly identify the trigger and the reasons why it affects you so much. You need to link it back to the past experience which it is related to and you need to let that experience go. Forgive anyone involved, forgive yourself, send love to everyone involved, and let it fly in the wind.

A good way to do this is actually visualisation. Write down the issue that is causing you the problem. Fold up the piece of paper and head outside. Take a lighter to that piece of paper and watch the flames eat away at it. As they do this, focus on the flames and feel the hurt and other emotions connected to the issue burn away too. By the time the piece of paper is nothing but a pile of ashes, you should feel lighter as a result.

Practising forgiveness and letting go of toxic and negative situations is a healthy way to deal with problems and allows you to grow as a result.

Take a Moment to Deal With Your Response

This strategy relies upon you being mindful. The next time you experience the trigger, acknowledge it and recognise it. Say to yourself "I am experiencing my trigger". If you can put the trigger into a few words, that would work well too.

Then, close your eyes and focus on your breathing. Breathe in through your nose for a count of five in a slow and steady manner. Pause for another count of five. Exhale through your mouth for the same slow count of five. Repeat until you feel calm. If you need to take yourself away from the situation in order to do this, that's a good idea.

Then, when you're ready, open your eyes and focus on the trigger. How do you feel now? It's likely that the emotions you felt before, or the emotions you've felt in the past, are far less now and you're able to control what you say and do more effectively.

The more you practice this technique, the easier it will become, and the faster you'll reach that calm state. This is also a technique you can use in many different situations, and it is very useful when anxiety strikes, or when you feel angry and you need a moment to calm down before reacting.

Reframe The Trigger

Later on in the book, we're going to talk about reframing as a positive mindset technique, however, in this context we're going to use it to relinquish the hold a trigger has over you.

Identify a specific trigger and then come up with an alternative story. For instance, if one of your triggers is a fear of being cheated on in a relationship, reframe that into something more positive. You could change it to contentment that you're in a relationship now. It can be anything, but you need to flip the trigger on its head so that it holds no negative intention towards you.

Then, repeat it a few times to settle it in your mind. The next time you experience that trigger, quickly repeat the new reframed version a few times and wait a few seconds to see how you feel. It's likely that the emotional impact will be far less and you'll be able to react in a healthier and more positive way as a result.

Points to Remember
From This Chapter

This chapter has been our first real practical element in helping you to take control of your emotions. This chapter has talked in detail about emotional triggers and what they mean to you. We've also covered several useful strategies to help you overcome your triggers over time.

It's certainly worth pointing out that one attempt at overcoming a trigger probably won't bring you great results. However, the more you do it, you'll see that practice really does make perfect. Consider these to be baby steps towards a brighter future.

The main points to remember from this chapter are:

- We all have emotional triggers and they're completely personal to us
- You will not share the same trigger with a friend or anyone close to you
- Some people have more triggers than others and that's fine
- It's a good idea to tackle one trigger at a time, to avoid overloading yourself
- Before you start trying to overcome triggers you first need to identify them. A journal is a good

option here or a brainstorming session. You could also ask the opinion of someone close to you

- Using strategies to overcome triggers takes time and it might take a few attempts before you notice a difference
- The point of overcoming a trigger isn't to completely erase it from your life, as there is a chance it will always hold some meaning to you, but to help reduce it and therefore give you more of a say in how you react to it.

Chapter 5:
How Your Lifestyle Affects Your Emotions

The next step in learning how to conquer your emotions is looking at your base. That means looking at your lifestyle and how you live your life.

If you want to gain any amount of control over the maelstrom of emotions you experience on a day to day basis, you need to work with the basics first. So, do you consider yourself to have a healthy lifestyle, or are there changes you could make?

Most people can hold their hands up to a few unhealthy habits that they could stand to change. For instance, do you smoke? Do you drink a little too much? Do you binge eat to deal with your emotions?

These are all common outlets for emotional disturbances, but they're not healthy ways to cope. It's far better to find healthy outlets for difficult emotions, such as exercise or focusing on work, than opting for methods that are going to cause you to enter into a vicious circle.

For instance, how do you think drinking too much actually helps you to deal with difficult emotions? Sure, for the first couple of drinks you'll probably feel better, distracted even, but after a few drinks the depressive side of alcohol will kick in. This will leave you wallowing in upset, questioning what you're doing, and basically creating a cycle of behaviour that has no exit route.

The same can be said for overeating. You might think it's relatively harmless, eating chocolate or other foods to deal with emotions that cause you upset, but what happens when you start to put weight on? You'll feel unhealthy within yourself, sluggish even, your clothes won't fit, and you'll start to have body image issues. As a result, you've created another issue for yourself that you could have avoided.

Identifying any unhealthy coping mechanisms is the first step towards changing your lifestyle for the better, but there is a bigger picture to look at too.

In this chapter, we're going to talk about lifestyle in general and how having a poor lifestyle, to begin with, can actually start to affect your emotions. We've touched upon it already to a degree, e.g. if you're drinking too much then you're creating a damaging cycle, and if you're eating too much you could cause yourself other problems on top of the ones you already have. We're also going to talk about how your emotions can affect your health, i.e. the physical and mental conditions they can cause.

What Does a Poor Lifestyle do For You?

For a moment, let's talk about health and wellbeing on a broader scale.

What do you consider a poor lifestyle to actually look like? We're talking about things like:

- Smoking
- Drinking excessively or binge drinking
- Drug taking
- An unhealthy diet
- Using food as a coping mechanism
- Not exercising regularly
- Not having enough quality sleep on a nightly basis
- Not taking care of your mental health, e.g. bottling problems up and not talking about them
- Working to excess
- Having a poor home and work-life balance
- Risky behaviour, such as careless sexual activity in order to mask a deeper feeling
- Not getting physical conditions and symptoms checked by a doctor

Now, it's important to understand that everyone is guilty of something when it comes to their lifestyle. Nobody on the planet has the perfect lifestyle without any downsides, but it's about moderation. For example, you can drink if you want to, but in moderation, and you can eat chocolate and other unhealthy foods if you want to, in moderation. However, when moderation goes out of the window, you have to start thinking a little more deeply about whether changes need to be made.

A poor quality lifestyle affects you in countless different ways. It makes you unhealthy on the inside, which shows on the outside. As a result, your confidence begins to tumble, and it starts to affect your mental health, with possible anxiety and depression creeping in. You start to use unhealthy coping mechanisms to deal with emotions that are difficult to face, and you enter into endless cycles of negativity as a result.

All of this comes from having an unhealthy lifestyle.

On the flip-side, when you start to focus on health and wellbeing and positive thinking, everything changes for the better.

This book is about controlling your emotions and dealing with your reactions to difficult emotions in a healthier way. However, you can't do any of that if you don't have the foundation on which to build. That means looking at your lifestyle and making changes where they need to be made.

Lifestyle Issues to Avoid You Want Control Over Your Emotions

So, where do you need to target your efforts?

As we've already mentioned, you can do many things which are considered unhealthy provided they're in moderation and not often. However, there are some things that should never be done, such as drug-taking. If you want to gain control over your emotions, you need to be strong on the inside, both physically and mentally. In order to achieve that, you need to avoid the following:

- **Smoking.** If you already smoke, work to cut down on the amount you smoke per day, and if you can, work towards stopping completely. Not only is smoking terrible for your general health, but it's also extremely expensive! You'll save a small fortune over the course of just one year if you quit, and you'll also notice that your health and wellbeing improves by a large amount. In terms of your emotions, that stronger foundation of health will allow you to be stronger mentally too, giving you more control over your emotional reactions.

- **Excessive drinking or binge drinking.** You can enjoy a drink every now and again, and you can drink socially, but if you're using drink as a crutch, or you're drinking too much, it's time to stop. If you're going to drink alcohol, drink it because you enjoy it occasionally and not because you either need it, you feel like you have to (peer pressure), or simply for the hell of it. Alcohol is a depressant and after a while, it's going to drag you down. When you're in that state, your emotions are going to be all over the place, and alcohol clouds your judgement. That means your emotional reactions are going to be far more 'out there' and extreme than they would be otherwise. You lose your ability to stop and think for a second before acting or speaking when you've been drinking. Look honestly at your drinking patterns and make changes if necessary.

- **Drug taking.** By this, we're not talking about the prescription medication that you take as prescribed by your doctor. We're talking about illegal drugs or any other type of substance that you use recreationally. There is a reason why drugs are controversial, and that's because they're dangerous and not at all healthy. In this case, you need to stop completely if you're someone who does use any type of drug in this way. Your emotions will not be under your own control when you're under the influence of any type of drug and over time drugs have been shown to have severe psychological effects. This means your emotions will be unpredictable and your ability to control your reactions will be out of the window. If you need help and support to stop taking any type of substance, take the brave step to reach out and get the help you need.

- **Overeating or having a generally unhealthy diet.** The foods you eat can actually cause you to have worse emotional reactions to problems. This is all down to stress hormones, and certain foods have been shown to affect stress hormones detrimentally. We're talking about things like processed meats and foods, too much caffeine, alcohol, etc. These types of foods raise the cortisol (stress hormone) level in your system and cause you to deal with your emotions differently. We're going to talk about stress a little more shortly, but when you're stressed dealing with emotions in a positive way can be very difficult. Instead, focus on healthy eating and getting the vitamins and minerals your body needs for overall health and wellbeing. If you find that you're overeating in order to deal with a difficult emotion, make a pact with yourself to tackle the problem rather than trying to mask it with binge eating.

- **Not placing priority on sleep.** It's 100% impossible to control your emotions or your reactions if you're sleep-deprived. Think back to the last time you had a bad night's sleep and how you felt the next morning. You were probably agitated, easily annoyed, snappy, and maybe even emotional. When you feel that way, you aren't strong enough physically or mentally to deal with emotions in a healthy way, and you're more likely to react in a negative way as a result. Adults are recommended to have between 7 to 8 hours of uninterrupted sleep every night. Avoid any unnecessary stimulation before bed, such as loud movies or music, using the computer or scrolling through social media.

- **Not dealing with problems or stressful situations.** When you bottle things up and don't face problems head-on, you're more likely to find yourself overwhelmed. This blocks your focus and leaves you at the mercy of difficult situations that you can't focus on in a healthy way. Instead of bottling emotions up and pushing them away, focus on dealing with them head-on instead. Use stress management techniques to handle anything which causes you to feel overwhelmed. When you place importance and priority on your mental health, you're in a much better space to deal with your emotions.

How Your Emotions Affect Your Health

Now we know that your health can affect your ability to handle your emotions and how you react, let's flip the situation around. How can your emotions actually affect your health?

It turns out, they can affect your health in a very severe way if you allow them to.

Constant negativity can cause you to feel helpless and extremely down. This leads to the possibility of depression and anxiety, which has been linked with its own list of health problems, including a risk of heart conditions, reduced immune system, and an increased risk of developing diabetes. Of course, we all know that living with depression and anxiety, either both or just one, is an extremely unpleasant experience and it's not something you should be inviting into your life.

In addition, negativity can actually cause a disruption in the body's hormone levels. An increase in stress hormones means tattle brain doesn't get enough of the hormones it requires for happiness, e.g. dopamine, serotonin, oxytocin, and endorphins. This can lead to poor immune system function, leaving you open to illness and disease.

When you look at it this way, giving in to your negative emotions can actually lead to extremely poor health and even the risk of death if one of the associated conditions worsens to the point of severity.

This isn't meant to cause you distress or worry; it's simply a case of stating a fact. When you allow your emotions to be constantly negative, when you do not handle situations well, and when you allow yourself to be dragged down into a pit of despair, the outlook is bleak for your physical and mental health.

Emotions are not merely feelings; they're an important part of a healthy lifestyle that contributes to the entire outlook of your life. Does that add impetus to the challenge of controlling your emotions?

It certainly should!

Points to Remember
From This Chapter

This chapter has been another of those cautionary tales. In our last chapter, we talked about identifying and minimising emotional triggers, but this chapter has reaffirmed why that needs to happen.

When you allow negative emotions to rule your life, they're also ruling your health. When you allow your health to become negative, you're looking at the possibility of extreme illness, both physically and mentally.

The main points to take from this chapter are:

- Emotions affect your health, both physically and mentally
- Your lifestyle can affect your emotions and your ability to handle them in a healthy way
- Unhealthy coping mechanisms, e.g. drinking, smoking, drug-taking, overeating, are all masks for your emotions and not a way of actually dealing with the core problem
- It is impossible to live a healthy and happy life if you're ruled by your emotions, however, when you gain control, you will find yourself happier and healthier almost by default.

Chapter 6:

Do You Constantly Feel Not Good Enough?

We live in demanding times. We're supposed to do everything, be everything, wear a million hats at any one time, and excel at all of it. We're supposed to look a certain way, act a certain way, be successful, be happy, and be healthy, whilst avoiding disaster.

We place a huge amount of pressure on ourselves, and we expect ourselves to live up to unrealistic targets.

When you think about it, is it any wonder that so many people have problems with self-esteem, depression, anxiety, and a lack of emotional control?

This chapter is going to talk about why the constant feeling of 'not being good enough' is ruining your life.

For starters, what exactly is 'good enough'? Good enough for what exactly? For who? And who decides what the elusive 'good enough' really is?

It's likely trying to chase the idea of perfection. Perfection doesn't exist, because what one person perceives to be perfect; another person thinks isn't enough. The same goes for trying to be 'good enough'. It's a personal opinion and that means you're never going to please everyone.

What you need to ask yourself, in that case, is why you want to please everyone in the first place!

How does this all link into your emotions? Easy. When you don't feel like you're good enough, you're in a cycle of negativity, and that means negative emotions will come your way with ease. You might turn to unhealthy coping mechanisms to handle the way you feel, and you're more likely to find yourself in the middle of an emotional outburst as a result of all of this.

All because you simply don't feel 'good enough'.

Why Comparisons Are Useless

At the end of the day, not feeling good enough comes down to comparing yourself to other people. We do this because we don't have any other measuring tool or yardstick. The only thing we can measure ourselves against is the standards and lives of others.

Why do you need to measure in the first place? Ask yourself that. It's far better to be happy with who you are, what you stand for, and work towards things which are healthy and of importance to you, than to tick a so-called perfection box which doesn't really mean anything.

It's all a total waste of your precious time.

Shortly we're going to talk about social media. Now, we're not placing the blame firmly at the feet of social media, but it certainly hasn't helped. It's far easier to compare yourself against other people when their lives are there for all to see on a social media platform.

The reason that comparing yourself to another person is just as much use as using chocolate as a fireguard is because you can never be sure what is going on beneath the surface.

For instance, someone may appear very happy on the outside. They might smile every day, wear the best clothes, laugh with ease, and always look well turned out. However, deep down inside, they might be crying themselves to sleep every night. They might turn to alcohol during the evening to cope with their feelings of inadequacy, and they might simply smile as a mask for their general unhappiness.

It's entirely possible, and you cannot tell any of this by simply looking at someone.

So, when you compare yourself to another person, you're comparing yourself against an image that may or may not even exist.

Nobody is happy all the time, nobody looks wonderful all the time, and nobody does the right thing all of the time. Our flaws are what make us human.

Comparisons and emotions are so closely linked that we have to explore this in some detail.

When you compare yourself to another person, it's very unlikely that you'll feel positive about it. Our human brains are naturally hard-wired towards the negative option before the positive, and without a fair amount of cognitive training to the contrary, this is your default setting. So when you compare yourself to another person, you're always going to come up short. Your brain will say "she has better eyes than me, her hair is better than mine, or he's always laughing, they're always successful". It won't think about your own positive traits.

So, how do you feel then? Inadequate.

It's a huge hammer blow to your confidence which leaves you open to even more negativity coming your way. Your ego kicks in, whispering damaging sweet nothings in your ear, and as a result, your emotions fire up.

You started feeling inadequate, but now you're kicking yourself, you're feeling angry, sad, jealous, shameful, the list goes on.

If you're unable to handle those emotions in a healthy way, you're open to reacting in a very unhealthy way instead. This could be an outburst that you don't mean, or turning to an unhealthy coping mechanism, such as smoking, drinking, drugs, overeating, etc.

All because you decided to compare yourself to another person.

The ironic thing is that the person you're comparing yourself to is probably doing the same to you, comparing themselves to you and coming up short in their own minds.

We're all guilty of it at some point, but the key to overcoming this dangerous behaviour is awareness.

The Potential Role of Social Media

Let's talk about social media for a second.

How often do you use Facebook, Twitter, Instagram, Snapchat, etc.?

Most of us use them daily at the very least, and usually numerous times per day.

Now, when you use social media for positive reasons, these platforms are actually very useful. You can stay in touch with people you don't get to see too often, read interesting articles that you enjoy, and you're able to appreciate the lives of others.

However, when you allow your interest in social media to become negative, e.g. comparisons, it can be very damaging indeed.

Let's just run through an example here, which highlights the illusion of social media very clearly.

Perhaps it's January, and you're feeling a little bloated from all the eating and drinking during the festive season. You're tired, bloated, probably lacking in cash until payday, and it's dark outside. It's understandable that you feel that way because most of us do during the first month of the year.

To pass the time, you sit on your sofa, and you scroll through Instagram. Your scrolling stops when you see a photo of a work colleague on a beautiful beach, looking radiant, with their partner behind them, beaming at the camera and looking utterly in love.

This can go one of two ways.

You can either smile at the photo and think how great they look, hitting 'like' and carrying on with your scrolling, or you can go down the damaging route.

Instead, you look at the photo and start to compare your situation to theirs. You're not on a beach, you're not looking radiant, you're not with your partner, and you're not beaming with happiness.

You suddenly feel very negative, very inadequate, and you have a sinking feeling in the pit of your stomach.

The truth of the matter is quite interesting.

Most people don't post the truth on social media. If they did, the entire platform of social media would be extremely boring indeed. The chances are, just before that photo was taken the couple had an argument and the beaming smile is as a result of trying too hard not to cry at the words they threw at each other. Two nights before they went out for a meal which left them both with crippling food poisoning for 24 hours afterwards, hence why they're looking quite svelte and not bloated.

You cannot know the truth from a photo, and that means you're comparing yourself to something which isn't real.

This is the truth of social media, and it's an example that we all see time and time again. It's far too easy to compare yourself to other people and come up short when the world is literally at your fingertips.

Why do you think social media influencers become so popular and make so much cash? Their entire career is based around making others feel so inadequate that they buy the product they're selling, attempting to reach the unrealistic target that is staring back at them.

Big business is made from making people feel inadequate, and by buying into it, you're damaging your own emotional health.

How to Challenge Your 'Not Good Enough' Mindset

If you regularly feel like you're just not good enough, it's time to challenge that mindset and turn it on its head.

The results aren't going to happen overnight, and it might take a little time before you start to notice results, but after a while, you will see that you feel a little more confident, a little stronger, and you don't feel the need to compare yourself to others quite so much. By doing this, you're creating a more positive mindset, you'll experience more positive emotions, and you'll be stronger and more able to deal with any negativity that comes your way as a result.

Here's how.

Write a List of Your Strong Points

Many people find this particular exercise quite difficult because they're so used to being self-deprecating and negative. We live in a society that tells us we should be humble and that 'bigging yourself up' is arrogant.

The truth is the total opposite!

Sit down with a pen and paper and write a list of all your positive points. This can be anything appearance-wise, personality-wise, outlook-wise, anything you can think of. Keep going until you can't think of anything else.

Now, choose five points from that list which you deem to be the most important. Focus on those points for a day and think about them carefully. The next day, choose a different five, and so on.

The hope is that over time, you start to notice your good points over your bad points. Everyone has negative traits, it's part of being human, but choosing to focus on the good over the bad is something which will boost your confidence, and allow you to deal with life's ups and downs in a healthier way. This also means that your emotions will be positive first and foremost.

Celebrate your strong points and stop telling yourself that you're 'not good enough'!

Use Positive Affirmations

The use of positive affirmations is ideal for many different situations, but it's ideal for rewiring your brain towards the positive and being able to focus on positive emotions, rather than negative ones.

A few examples of affirmations which may help you gain control over your emotions are:

- "I am strong, and I am in control"
- "I control the way I feel"
- "The control is in my hands"
- "I am able to deal with anything"
- "I will prevail"

You get the picture.

Once you find an affirmation that you associate with strength, you need to repeat it until it becomes engrained in your mind. Write it down, stick it somewhere prominent, and repeat it three times when you wake up, three times at another point during the day and then three times before bed. Whenever you feel yourself starting to feel negative or you notice that emotions are bubbling up, repeat it again. Eventually, your brain will start to firmly believe what you're telling it.

Go on a Social Media Detox

We've already talked about the fact that social media can be damaging if you allow comparisons to take over your life. If you feel that's the case for you, go on a social media detox and don't use it for a while.

For some people, this can be difficult. Social media addiction is a very real thing, but that's all the more reason to detox your life a little.

Log out of your social media accounts for one week and do not access them during this time. It might be difficult at times but try and distract yourself. After a few days, you might find that you forget about it completely.

Once the week is over, assess how you feel. Do you want to look at your news feeds or do you think you can detox a little more? Stay away from social media for as long as you feel you need to. When you want to log back in, so do in a controlled manner.

This means limiting your exposure to social media from this point onwards. Give yourself an hour a day, and make sure it's not the first thing you do once you wake up or before you sleep. If you feel like you're starting to make comparisons once more, repeat the process and detox for another week.

Points to Remember
From This Chapter

Practising self-love is not something most of us find easy to do. We feel like we're 'big-headed' if we talk about our plus points, but it's actually something we should all be doing. Why not celebrate yourself?

This chapter has talked about the dangers of comparisons and why most of us feel like we're just not good enough. This has a very dangerous effect on our emotional control because we're allowing a negative mind-set to establish itself.

The main points to take from this chapter are:

- Not feeling good enough is common, but that doesn't mean its acceptable
- What is 'good enough' anyway? Comparing yourself to other people basically means that you're comparing yourself to an illusion - you never know what is going on beneath the surface
- Social media makes it easier to compare yourself to others, so a social media detox is often a good idea
- Learning that you are good enough for yourself is the route towards strength and happiness, and this will allow you to deal with emotions in a more positive way.

Chapter 7:

How to Develop a Positive Mindset

Our brains are hard-wired towards the negative side of the scale first and foremost. You could argue that the human race is a pretty negative bunch, but we can change that!

Negativity is damaging in many different ways. If you allow negativity to take over your life, your health and wellbeing will take a nose dive pretty quickly. We've already mentioned several times that negative emotions are hard to deal with and if you allow them to take control over your life, you'll have no say over your reactions or your words as a result. However, that doesn't have to be the case.

In this chapter, we're going to focus on total positivity. You might wonder how that links into controlling your emotions, but that will become abundantly clear. The bottom line is this - if you're positive, you have a greater sense of purpose, you can see things far clearer, the bigger picture is in front of you, and everything is easier to deal with as a result.

That doesn't mean that you're never going to experience negative emotions or go through hard times in your life, of course, you still will, but you'll have the tools and the calmness to be able to deal with them far more effectively, and they won't drag you down to the depths as they probably do at the moment.

This is a positive and practical chapter. It's a good idea to be open and honest about whether or not you're a negative or positive person right now. The fact that you're reading this book probably means that you're not the sunniest of people, but that's fine; everyone has their bad days, and everyone struggles occasionally. What we're asking right now however, is that you take a moment to look for the sun in the clouds, and when you focus on it, it becomes brighter over time.

How Does Positivity Help You Manage Your Emotions?

We've already talked about the fact that not being able to control your emotions, or allowing your emotions to control you, has a very detrimental impact on your health. We've also mentioned that negativity is linked to several different health conditions. So, can you turn that around by changing your mindset? For sure!

Becoming a more positive person takes time, and it's not something you're going to notice overnight. Remember, your default setting is negative, and if you want to change that setting, you need to do a little rewiring. In this chapter, we're going to talk about three specific strategies you can try to alter your setting from negative to positive. One of them in particular, called reframing, is a recognised cognitive behavioural therapy treatment (CBT) that is used to help in treatment for various different mental health conditions.

So, how does being more positive help you take hold of the reins on your emotions?

Because when you're positive, you have more control. When you're positive, negative emotions still occur, of course, but they're not as extreme, and they don't have the same strength as they do right now. In your mind and in your body, you're also stronger, and your outlook gives you a certain amount of protection from the maelstrom of emotions that threatens to bubble up whenever a trigger comes your way.

Of course, being positive overall isn't going to help you control your emotions alone, but it will go along way to helping. You need to focus on your triggers, identify them and find ways to minimise them at the same time, but being more positive in general will certainly give you a huge advantage over your emotions.

In addition, when you have a more positive mindset, you are open to different solutions to problems, and you're generally more resilient emotionally too.

We're now going to talk about three ways you can focus on trying to become more positive. However, we should point out that all three of these techniques require you to be open-minded and to put forth the effort. It takes time and hard work to change your mind-set. Remember, you've been thinking the same way for x number of years, so changing that isn't going to happen overnight! It will happen, however, provided you're committed to the change. By making it this far in the book, you've shown that you're open to that already.

The Art of Positive Affirmations

A little earlier in the book, we touched upon positive affirmations, but in terms of changing your mindset from negative to positive, these affirmations are extremely useful.

Positive affirmations are ideal for boosting confidence and helping you to believe in something, so it stands to reason that they're going to do the same for changing your outlook towards the positive end of the scale.

The key to making positive affirmations work for you is to choose an affirmation that you really feel, something which resonates deep within your soul. You can't just choose any old affirmation and expect it to work. If you choose something which doesn't really mean anything to you, you can repeat it as many times as you like but it won't be as effective as if you choose something which really resonates. Your mind isn't stupid; it wants something it believes in!

In terms of becoming a more positive person, you could think about affirmations such as:

- "I am above negative thoughts and actions"
- "Today I choose positivity"
- "My thoughts are positive, and I am thankful"

- "I am strong, I am able, I am undefeated"
- "I am strong enough to handle whatever will come my way"
- "I radiate light and positivity"

Again, you get the picture.

Once you find an affirmation you like, or you've made up your own, you need to have it somewhere visible. If you work in an office, write your affirmation down on a piece of paper and stick it to your computer monitor. You could also stick it on the refrigerator door, or you could place it on the bathroom mirror, so it's the first thing you see in the morning. Additionally, you could set it as the background image on your phone. It just needs to be easily visible.

Now you need to repeat it. Repetition is key because our brains learn via repetition. It is for this reason your teacher made you sing the alphabet song over and over again when you were small. This wasn't because she was being annoying, it was because the repetition of singing this song committed it to your long term memory bank and you know for sure, without any wavering doubt, that the alphabet is exactly as you learnt it. The same needs to happen with your affirmation.

So, when you wake up in the morning, you need to repeat your positive affirmation three times. This doesn't have to be the moment you open your eyes, but as soon afterwards as you can. You also need to repeat it periodically throughout the day, at least two times and again before bed. If you can say the word aloud that will work best, but if you're not in a space where chanting a repetitive affirmation is socially acceptable, then in your mind is good enough. All you need to do is concentrate on the words and really listen to them, allowing them to vibrate through your body and focus on believing them.

At first, it will feel like you're just saying words, but the more you focus on them and the more you truly believe the weight of the meaning, the more power those words will have. Then, when you're feeling a little down, or perhaps you're having a day when negativity is threatening to win, repeat your affirmation a few more times, to banish the negativity away and replace it with strength and positivity.

What is Reframing?

Reframing is a very useful and successful CBT method that takes a negative thought and replaces it with a positive one. You then use repetition to set the new thought in your mind and kick the old one out.

The problem with reframing is that it is very time consuming and takes a lot of effort but the results are extremely beneficial, so it's more than worth it. You need to be aware of every negative thought you're having, which can be difficult at first. If you're so used to being negative, it can be hard to acknowledge when negativity is present in your mind. So, if you want to use reframing (and it's a good idea to try) you need to be very mindful of your thoughts throughout the day. This may mean that you're not quite as sociable, because you're so self-absorbed, but it's for a good reason. You might want to explain this to your nearest and dearest, so you don't upset anyone!

Reframing goes a little like this:

• When a negative thought enters your mind, acknowledge it and label it as negative. For example, if it's raining and the first thing that pops into your mind is "I hate rain", you need to acknowledge that thought as negative. Remember, this is just a simple example; it can be any type of thought.

- Now you know the thought is negative and therefore not useful to you, you need to change it to something positive. This is the reframing part of the techniques. So, instead of "I hate rain", it could be something like "the smell of rain is so refreshing". Again, this is just a random example. Tell yourself 'this is a positive thought'.

- Focus on the rain and repeat the positive thought three times. It's best to say it aloud, but again, you can do it in your head if that's easier for you at that moment in time.

- Wait a few seconds and then repeat the positive thought another three times, whilst picturing how refreshing the rain is.

- Congratulate yourself on being more positive.

- The next time you notice the rain, it could be that you first come up with a negative thought, but it should be quickly replaced again by the positive. Your brain will start to associate rain with being refreshing over time, and the more you repeat your positive thought, the more your brain will accept that to be the truth.

You need to be mindful of the thoughts that enter your brain throughout the day and complete this process for all the major ones. Don't worry about every single thought you have, just pick out the ones which you feel are significant and focus on those. Over time you will start to notice that the positive replaced throughs pop into your mind far quicker and eventually will be your go-to default setting.

Why Mindfulness Can be a Useful Positivity Tool

Our final positivity enhancing method is mindfulness.

Mindfulness is a fantastic way to become more positive, but also to help you live firmly in the moment. Most of us tend to either live in the past or jump forward to the future, and that stops us from enjoying the moment we're in. The problem is, if you're always rewinding or fast-forwarding, you're missing out on the joy of the present and you'll end up living to regret it, which is another breeding ground for lost time and negativity.

Mindfulness can be as easy or as difficult as you want it to be, but because we're dealing with a bigger picture here, e.g. how to control your emotions, we'll keep this part of the equation simple.

Learning to live in the present day helps you feel calmer and more enlightened, and as a result, you'll find negative emotions less troublesome. When you're mindful, you're not actually absorbed in the moment per se, but you're more of an observer. You're feeling it and you're enjoying it, but you're viewing the bigger picture. That means when you're in the middle of a negative situation, or you're feeling something adverse, you can almost float above it and let it go, rather than allowing it to consume you.

As you can see, mindfulness is both a tool for controlling emotions and also for becoming more positive as a happy side effect.

So, how can you practice mindfulness? The simplest way is as follows:

- Head outside for a walk on your own. If you can choose somewhere quiet in the middle of nature, that's even better
- Make sure you're wearing comfortable clothes and that you're not distracted by your phone. Don't wear earphones or listen to music; you need to be in the moment as it is
- As you walk, focus on your breathing and feel your chest rising and falling. As you do so, you'll start to feel calmer
- When you feel calm and in control, observe what is going on around you. Look at the trees and the way the leaves blow in the wind, listen to the gentle hiss of the breeze, and notice the colours of the grass. Focus on the smaller details and really appreciate them
- Keep concentrating until you start to feel tired, but make sure you're really taking in the details, rather than just looking at them fleetingly

- Repeat this process a few times every week, making it an enjoyable part of your routine

The more you do this, the more you will notice smaller details and the more you'll become used to being right at the moment. You're not on your phone, you're not talking to anyone, you're not scrolling through social media, and you're not distracted by music, you're right in the middle of the moment you're in, and you're enjoying it.

Noticing these small details will give you a greater appreciation of what is around you, and that in itself helps you to become more upbeat and positive in general. You could also take this a step further and write a 'thankful diary'. This means every single day you write down something you're thankful for, something which you noticed during your mindfulness practice. This will help you become more open and positive in life.

Again, mindfulness is something that takes time. Many people take this a step further and go into meditation with it, but if you are short on time or you find it hard to focus for long periods of time, start with the exercise above and see where it takes you first.

Points to Remember
From This Chapter

This chapter has been an upbeat and positive one!

Having a more positive mindset will help you to focus and control your emotions, simply because you're stronger and more able to deal with whatever life throws at you. Positivity helps you in your health, but it also allows you to see more creative solutions to issues, cutting out the panic and negativity which often works hand in hand when someone is unable to take control of their emotions.

The main points to take from this chapter are:

- Positive thinking can help you become healthier, happier, and can also help you deal with and control your emotions far more effectively
- Becoming a more positive person takes time. You're basically rewiring your brain so you need to put forth the effort and allow yourself time
- Repetition is key with any mindset training, as this is how the brain learns new concepts and thought patterns
- Positive affirmations are a great way to rewire your brain towards the positive end of the spectrum
- Reframing is the art of taking an acknowledged negative thought and replacing it with something positive

- Mindfulness is a way to learn how to control your emotions, but also to help you become more positive in general.

Chapter 8:

How to Effectively Journal Your Emotions

In our chapter on emotional triggers, we briefly touched upon a very useful method of emotional trigger identification, called journalling. This chapter is going to go into more detail on that subject and help you to start journaling for yourself.

Everyone knows what a journal is. If you watch any teen drama on TV you'll know that journals are often the cause of major issues when someone reads another person's journal and spills all their secrets! For that reason, it's a good idea to keep your journal somewhere private and perhaps invest in a lock. We're not suggesting anyone in your life is going to read your journal, but the security side of things will give you more confidence and allow you to be freer in what you write down.

All you need is a notebook, a pen and a willingness to explore your own emotional triggers and patterns. The information you will learn by using this method will allow you to become enlightened on the things which press your emotional buttons, and as a result, you'll find it far easier to work towards controlling what you feel.

First things first, let's define the emotional journey method completely and give you a full rundown of what it is, and what it most definitely isn't.

What is an Emotions Journal?

An emotions journal is basically a record of how you feel on any specific day. Shortly we're going to talk about how you actually go about journaling your emotions, but for now, let's make sure you're clear on how to use this type of method.

Firstly, a journal and a diary are two separate things. A diary is more about scheduling, e.g. writing down the things you need to do and when bills are coming out of your bank account! A journal, on the other hand, is your own personal thoughts, musings, and feelings, and this allows you to declutter your mind on a daily basis.

From that, you can understand that an emotions journal is actually a two-pronged benefit. Firstly, you're allowing yourself to have a deeper insight into what your emotional triggers are, by analysing what you've written and looking for patterns, and secondly, you're downloading all the information you've dealt within a day and clearing out your mind.

Sometimes, the basic action of writing things down can be very cathartic. When you write down how you're feeling, the pen is likely to flow across the paper quite easily. Before you know it, you've written what seems like an essay, and by the end, you feel much better, lighter even.

Writing down your feelings is a form of therapy and can allow you to get rid of pent up emotions. When you allow your emotions to build and you don't release them, they're just going to explode at some point; this will probably be a very badly timed point that doesn't help you or the people around you at the time.

For instance, if you're feeling a little unsure of something in your relationship and you're bottling up how you feel, you will be fine for so long, but at some point, your partner will say something without meaning anything, and you'll blow. From that, all the worries and concerns will flow out, but they won't come out in a healthy way, they'll come out in a stream of accusations and concerns that probably cause your partner to recoil in horror.

Bottling up emotions is a fast-track to bad reactions, but writing them down is a good way to release them. Of course, talking about your emotions is a better option, but if you don't want to share your thoughts and feelings, or you simply want to sort through your ideas and thoughts without voicing them, journaling is a great way to go about it.

Remember, this journal is for your eyes only, and that means you're free to write you want. If you want to rant and rave for your own therapy, then go for it if it makes you feel better. By writing down your emotions, you're freeing them from your own mind and you're making sense of them too. When you write something down, you unpick it, analyse it and you start to question whether or not what you're writing about is really all that important.

For instance, perhaps something happened at work that day, and you've returned home quite angry about it. Maybe you had an argument with a colleague because you feel like they stole your idea. This type of situation can be very damaging to work relations because arguments in the workplace are never a good idea. If you can manage to control your anger in that moment and make it home without saying anything, you did well.

However, at home, you can take your journal somewhere quiet and write down your feelings and your take on what happened. Get it all out. Then, wait an hour and go back to read it. The chances are, when you read it back and you've had time to calm a little, you'll start to see that the issue really isn't as earth-shattering as you first thought it was. In some ways, you might even read back the events as you've written them and see how ridiculous it all was.

Journalling is useful on so many levels, but there is a right way to do it and a wrong way. Let's explore that a little more now.

How to Journal Your Emotions

So, how do you actually journal how you feel?

Everyone will have their own personal way of writing their journal, so it's not for us to give you a how-to guide. However, there are a few guidelines that will help you get the best out of the experience, and a few things you should avoid doing.

Don't Try to Impress Anyone

Firstly, don't write your journal as though someone else is going to read it. This isn't an exercise to impress anyone with your writing skills, it's meant to be a form of therapy for you alone, something to help you identify your emotional triggers, release the emotional baggage of the day, and make sense of things in your own way.

That means you shouldn't censor what you want to write, you should basically write as though you're thinking aloud. Whatever comes into your mind, write it down, and if you want to do this in a conversational way, that will work too. It doesn't have to be paragraphs and perfect grammar, it can literally be a series of bullet points, keywords, even a mind map if that helps you. Whatever format you want to use should be the one you go with.

Use a Pen and Paper, Rather Than a Laptop or Computer

If you want to use a laptop or a computer and type what you feel, that's fine for you, but it's generally better to use a pen and paper and go down the old fashioned route. The reason is that when you write the words, you're forming them with your hand and allowing the words to flow from your brain, down your arm, and out of your fingers. The physical act of writing helps you to really feel what you're writing and allows you to decode your emotions and the events of the day in a deeper way.

It's almost like you're relieving the emotion again, feeling it as you write about it, and you can experience this far more effectively if you're physically writing the words, rather than typing them. However, if you have no choice or you simply don't want to spend time writing, then typing is far better than nothing!

Keep Your Journal Somewhere Safe

We've already touched upon this, and whilst it's very unlikely that anyone's going to look for your journal and read it, you'll feel more comfortable and freer to write what you want if you keep your journal somewhere safe and secure.

If you want to keep it with you at all times, just keep it in your bag, or place it in a drawer at the side of your bed. Wherever is safest for you and somewhere you're not going to lose it, is the ideal option.

How Often Should You Write?

At the start of your emotional control journey, it's best to write in your journal every day. This will give you the most information on what your personal emotional triggers are, and will help you to start your journey with all the tools you need. However, that doesn't mean if you miss a day the whole thing is ruined.

Find your ideal rhythm and work with that. As we've stated time and time again already, everyone is individual and that means you need to find the frequency of writing in a journal that works best for you. At the start, however, every day should be your aim, just until you get into the swing of things and you start to recognise your own triggers.

What to Write

The most obvious question is obviously, what should you write? Again, it's up to you! You can write your journal however you want to, but you simply need to make sure that you cover the key informational points. These are:

- The date you wrote the entry, so make sure you date it
- Bullet points or keywords of the main emotions you felt. Try and put a name to them if you can as this will help you identify triggers more easily
- The events which surrounded or led up to you feeling that emotion

You can put as much detail into it as you want to, but the more you write, the more information you'll have. As long as you cover the three main points above, there are no other real guidelines on how to write your journal. If you want to write more and you feel like you want to go off on a rant about the day's events, that's fine! Remember, part of journaling is for your own cathartic therapy too, so write away until you feel like you've got everything out! Some days, however, you might simply want to write bullet points and a few keywords - that's equally as fine.

Your journal is a personal and very private thing, so it really comes down to you finding your own groove in terms of how you write it and how often. However, the advice we've given above should help you to get started with your journalling, and from there you can find the route that suits you best.

How to Find Trends or Patterns

After a while, you need to read back over your journal and look for patterns or trends. This will give you the information you need in order to identify your triggers. It's up to you how long you leave it before you review your journal, but make sure you don't try and look for information too soon, as you won't be able to identify patterns very easily. In general, it's best to wait at least two weeks before having your first sit down review of what you've written.

Once you do this, prepare for at least an hour or two of analysing work. Make sure you're comfortable and you're not going to be disrupted. You'll also need another piece of paper and a pen, so you can scribble a few notes down and identify your triggers.

Start at day one and write down the emotions that you felt, make a list as you go through and place a tick at the side whenever you notice that emotion repeated more than once. By the end, you'll be able to easily see the emotions that you experience on a regular basis. Perhaps you notice that you've been feeling angry quite often lately because you can see six or seven ticks at the side of the word 'angry'.

There will probably be more than one emotion you can identify as commonplace, so it might be that you've been feeling angry often lately, jealous, but maybe you've also been happy quite often too.

At this point, you'll only know the emotions by name, and you won't know what caused them. Now, you need to look a little deeper.

Choose one emotion at a time from your commonly felt like. So, choose anger first. Go through the days when you felt angry and look at the reasons why. It might be easier to write them down at this point so you don't become confused as you're working out the main reasons. Is there one particular reason for your anger which has occurred more than once? If so, that's a trigger for you. It might not be a long term trigger, but it's a trigger for you at a specific moment in time, i.e. at this stage in your life. You'll only know whether it is a long term trend if you journal for a longer period of time and notice the same pattern emerging. That might be something you want to do.

It could very well be that there are several different reasons for your anger, but can you see if there is a link between them? Are they associated in any way? Do they revolve around one person or a group of people? Do they revolve around work? Personal life? Can you group them together in any way?

Play around with ideas and look for trends. You might be on the right track, you might have fallen off the track a little but at least you'll have ideas to observe over the coming days.

An emotions journal isn't going to give you answers immediately, but it will show you where to look and give you suspicions which you can explore further.

Using The Information
You Have Learnt

Over a longer period of time, you'll certainly begin to see a more accurate pattern of what your emotional triggers are. For instance, you might see that anything related to an old relationship tends to bring up feelings of jealousy or regret. You might notice that anything related to a person who you work with, tends to make you feel tense or competitive. You might even notice that anything related to body image or appearance makes you feel shameful or lacking.

The longer you keep your journal, the more beneficial it will be.

So, what do you do with that information?

In our chapter on triggers we talked about the options you have in front of you, e.g. face the trigger head-on, minimise your exposure or avoid it completely. Which of these is suitable for each of the triggers you've identified?

It's far better to face a trigger and overcome it or at least reduce its impact on you than it is to completely try and avoid it. By avoiding it, you're simply running away from the problem. However, in some cases, this might be the best or only option you have. Weigh up the pros and cons of each when you have solid evidence of a personal emotional trigger.

Of course, you can also use the information you've learnt in your journal to help you do more of the things you enjoy. Perhaps you never realised that spending time outside makes you feel calm or even joyful, but it appears several times in your journal. That information will allow you to do more of that activity and therefore increase the calmness and joy in your life, working hand in hand with your efforts to be more positive in general.

An emotional journal isn't just to give you information on negative emotions, it's also to show you the things that make you happy, so you can work towards doing more of them.

Points to Remember
From This Chapter

In this chapter, we've covered a lot of information about emotion journals. No, you're not going back to your teenage or school years here, you're doing something which is worthwhile for you and something which will give you important information on what your potential triggers are.

Remember, your journal is a private series of notes that only you should read. Knowing this, and keeping your journal safe and out of reach of others will help you to feel more confident and freer to write with abandon.

The main points to remember from this chapter are:

- An emotions journal is a book which you use to record your daily emotions and the events which led up to them
- The primary reason for keeping a journal is to identify triggers which lead to regular emotions you experience
- By identifying triggers you can work towards minimising or possibly even reducing the effect they have on your life
- It's a good idea to write in your journal every day at the start, to help solidify your efforts

- It's best to write on paper rather than type on a computer screen, but this isn't out of the question
- Journals can be used as a therapy as well as a trigger identification method
- Review your journal after two weeks and see how you're doing, but remember to review it regularly after that to continue your good work.

Chapter 9:
The Art of Breathing

There are very few things in life that are static and still. Most things move around us, swirling, ever-changing, never staying still or pausing for breath. It can be very difficult to stay grounded when everything around you is constantly shifting and changing.

Change is something which many people find unnerving, in fact, you might find that change is one of your own personal emotional triggers. When things are always changing, you never feel in control, you might feel anxious a lot of the time, maybe even nervous and you feel like you just start to feel comfortable and the tables turn once more.

The good news is that there is one thing in your life that will never change. There is one thing which you can always move back towards whenever you feel like everything is moving too fast, or whenever you feel like your emotions are about to burst and spiral out of control.

We are of course talking about your breathing.

Breathing is easy. It's something you do unconsciously, something you do every single second of the day without even thinking or trying. Despite its ease, it's something that has extreme power.

Think about it - this easy motion, this thing you do without even thinking about it, it keeps you alive. If you stop breathing, you did. It's that simple.

Breathing is power and it can be used for more than simple survival. You can use the power and stillness of your breath to pull you back into the moment when you feel like your emotions are rising, or when you feel like you need a second to regroup and stop yourself from reacting in a way you would rather not. In addition, breathing is a great way to calm anxiety and stop yourself from overthinking everything at a million miles an hour.

Overthinking is one of the main causes of unhappiness and it has roots in your emotions. When you overthink something, your emotional responses kick in because you're thinking about things that you're fearful of. This is normally associated with the phrase "what if".

"What if" does you no good, because by thinking that way you're in the future, living in fear of what may come your way. The thing is, it might never come your way, so you've wasted precious time in the present worrying about something useless. When you do this, your emotions also rise because they respond to that fear. It's your fight or flight stress response turning itself on, preparing to keep you safe from a threat that you've convinced yourself is about to occur in the near future.

There is no threat. You've just created it and brought it to life in your imagination only.

Breathing can help you control all of this, and its something which is free, and something which you have an abundance of.

How Focusing on Breathing Helps You Control Your Emotions

So how does the simple action of breathing help you to be more in control of your emotions?

It all comes down to distraction and focusing on the thing which never changes. It's grounding and that pulls you back into the present and stops you from acting out.

When you focus on your breathing you're focusing on something natural, something automatically calming. The rhythm of your breathing helps you to block out everything around you and allows you to give yourself a few minutes to overcome the rise of your emotions. When you finally bring yourself back into the moment, the emotion has lost some of its strength, and you can stop yourself from reacting quite so strongly, if at all.

From a psychological point of view, studies have shown that when you focus on your breathing and control it, e.g. slow it down, you're activating parts of your brain that control the resting processes in your body. These are known as the parasympathetic processes. As a result, you're calmer and able to overcome the moment you're in.

When you are experiencing heightened emotions, your breathing changes. In our next section, we're going to talk about the proper way to breathe. You might think that sounds ridiculous because breathing is a natural thing, but most of us actually breathe from the wrong place!

So, when you're feeling angry or jealous, and your emotions are rising, it's likely that your rate of breathing accelerates alongside it. You'll start to breathe faster, perhaps in a more shallow way. As a result, you feel panicky, because you can't grab hold of the thing which normally grounds you, that feels like it's moving too fast or out of control too.

The key is to recognise that this is a normal occurrence and part of your emotional reaction. Once you know that, you can work to control your breath using deep breathing exercises. Again, we're going to talk about those shortly. Once you do these exercises, your breathing will slowly return to normal, you will feel calmer, and the heightened emotion will no longer hold the same control over you at that moment.

Do You Breathe Properly?

We just mentioned that most people don't actually breathe properly, but what does that mean?

Just for a second stop and turn your attention to your breath. Where are you breathing from? Do you feel it in your chest, your stomach, or a little lower down? Which part of your chest rises and falls on the inhalation and exhalation?

If you feel it in your chest, your stomach, or any higher than that, your breathing is shallow and therefore incorrect. The correct way to breathe is from your diaphragm. This is just below your breast bone, below your heart and your lungs. When you inhale, you should feel the air going right down into the depths of your stomach.

The two main types of breathing we're talking about here are known as thoracic breathing, i.e. breathing from your chest (shallow breathing), and diaphragmatic breathing (abdominal breathing). It is the latter you are aiming for.

If you find that you're breathing from the wrong place, the good news is that you can train yourself to be more mindful of your breathing and correct it. It actually doesn't take too long to change your breathing process, quite surprisingly! All you need to do is be more aware and try and do it in the right way.

To breathe properly, you need to follow these easy steps:

- Inhale through your nose and not your mouth
- Allow your diaphragm to rise with the inhale and feel the air going right down into the stomach
- Feel relaxed as you're doing this, it shouldn't be a tense or focused activity
- Exhale deeply through your nose
- Make sure you're breathing in a slow and rhythmic way, and it should be silent (unless you have a cold, of course!)

That is what good quality breathing looks like. If you're breathing fast and you haven't been exerting yourself, you need to slow things down. If you're breathing from the wrong place, you're not allowing the process to run as it should, and you might not be allowing nutrients to arrive where they're supposed to, or quite so effectively via the delivery of oxygen. You're also contributing to the anxiety or panic of the moment.

The effects of breathing incorrectly aren't catastrophic for your health per se, but they aren't going to help you when it comes to feeling more in control of your emotions. If you want to use breathing as an anchor and a safe place to control what you're feeling, you need to be doing it in the right way in the first place!

However, you might even find that if you're breathing too fast or too shallow, your body is in a constant state of stress awareness. Shallow and fast breathing is part of the fight or flight stress response, and that is another reason to focus on breathing correctly - being in a constant state of stress is not good for your health and wellbeing.

Easy Deep Breathing Exercises to Try

Now we know that breathing can be used as a good emotional control technique, how exactly can you use it? Let's look at some very easy deep breathing exercises you can use on the go.

Exercise 1

The easiest technique is a simple one that can be used whenever you need five minutes to yourself, or you feel like you're becoming overwhelmed and stressed, and you want to focus on calming down.

- Close your eyes and turn your attention to your breathing
- Breathe in through your nose for a count of five, keeping the count slow and steady
- Pause for a count of three
- Exhale through the mouth for a count of five, in the same slow and steady manner
- Pause for a count of three and repeat until you feel calm and in control

The good news is that you can use this technique anywhere and at any time. If you don't want to stand there with your eyes closed and focusing on your breathing in public, take yourself somewhere quiet and do it. You don't have to close your eyes if you don't want to, but the stillness will help you control your breathing more easily. An alternative is to focus on something still, i.e. a tree or something which isn't moving, such as a wall.

Exercise 2

This next exercise is very useful for anxious moments and it's best done when you're lying down; however, it's also possible to perform this exercise standing or sitting, if lying down at that moment isn't possible.

- Lay down and make yourself comfortable
- Close your eyes or focus on the ceiling above you
- Inhale deeply through your nose
- Make sure that your entire body is relaxed as you do so
- Turn your attention to your abdomen (diaphragm) and be mindful of it rising up
- Slowly breathe out through your mouth but as you do so, purse your lips a little and make a sound, such as a 'whoosh'. This is an audio acknowledgement of your breaths leaving your body
- Pause for a second and repeat until you feel calm.

Exercise 3

If you're about to encounter something you know is going to make you nervous or affect your emotions in some way, i.e. a personal trigger, you can try this very effective breathing exercise.

- Sit somewhere comfortable and make sure you're not going to be disturbed
- Place a hand on your chest
- Place the other hand on your lower abdomen
- Breathe in slowly through your nose and focus on the hand on your abdomen rising
- Be mindful that the hand on your chest doesn't rise
- Inhale to the point where you can feel that your lungs are full, e.g. there is a slight stretching feeling in your chest (lungs)
- Exhale through your nose, making sure that you do so in a slow and steady way

The idea is to get to the point where you're breathing no more than 10 times in one minute. At first, this is going to be difficult, especially if you're used to breathing in a shallow way, or you're feeling particularly stressed or anxious. Practice this exercise every day for around two months and see if you can reach the target.

Exercise 4

Our next exercise has roots in yoga and is known as 'Nadi Shodhana'. You might also hear it referred to as 'alternate nostril breathing'. This particular breathing exercise is great for dealing with stress or simply when you're feeling a little overwhelmed. In terms of your emotions, you could use this technique if you know that you're about to face a trigger.

- Sit somewhere comfortable and cross your legs if possible. Make sure that you're not going to be disturbed
- For this exercise, you need to use your dominant hand, so if you're right-handed, use that and if you're left-handed, use your left

- Bend the middle finger and pointing finger into the palm of your hand, but leave the other fingers straight
- Using your extended thumb, press against the side of one nostril (your dominant side) and breathe in deeply through the open nostril on the other side
- Once you get to the point where you feel a stretch in your lungs, i.e. you've inhaled as much as you can, move your thumb and move your extended ring finger to the opposite nostril, pressing against it
- Exhale slowly through the now released other nostril
- Repeat for 2 minutes on your dominant side and then switch sides so that you inhale and exhale in equal amounts through both sides

Exercise 5

Our final exercise is a very energetic one which is ideal for shaking off negativity and getting away from emotions that are causing you distress at the moment. You will hear this exercise called 'Kapalabhati' or maybe 'skull shining breath'. You might also like to do this exercise when you wake up in the morning, simply to give you a boost of energy.

- Sit on a chair with your back straight and your hands loosely resting on your knees
- Breathe in through your nose to the point where you feel a slight stretch in your lungs
- When you're ready, push the air out through your nose powerfully. You do this by pushing with the muscles of your abdomen
- Repeat

The aim here is to get to one inhale and exhale lasting for two seconds and to repeat it ten times in a cycle. The power of pushing out each breath through your abdomen will be a great distraction technique from difficult emotions, but it's also a way to push out negativity, especially if you visualise it as you do so.

Points to Remember
From This Chapter

This chapter has focused on breathing as an anchor and a way to control difficult emotions. Your breath is something solid which you can rely on, something which will never leave you or desert you, at least not whilst you're living anyway!

By using your breathing, you can take the focus away from triggers and emotions which cause you concern and avert the likelihood of acting out and saying or doing something you regret. We've covered a few different breathing techniques also, and whilst they're all very useful, it's likely that you'll have a favourite or two that you rely upon over time. That's fine, but at least try all five to see which one works best for you.

The main points to remember from this chapter are:

- Breathing is a solid and static thing in your life, i.e. it's always going to be there. As a result, you can use it as an anchor to deal with emotions
- Most people don't breathe correctly, and often use thoracic breathing (chest breathing) rather than diaphragmatic breathing (abdominal). This is something you can recognise and change
- Thoracic breathing can actually contribute to feelings of panic or anger, so learning how to

breathe from your diaphragm is a way to control your emotions on its own

- Different breathing techniques suit different people, but finding your own favourite options will give you tools to us whenever you feel like your emotions are about to rise
- Overthinking is a fast route towards difficult emotions, but breathing exercises can help to turn attention back to the present and avoid 'what if' thoughts.

Chapter 10:

Focus on Yourself And Get a Grip on Your Emotions

So far, you've learnt quite a few ways to start handling your emotions and learning to take back control, but sometimes the basics are just as powerful. You already know that you need to look after your health and wellbeing, but what about your mind?

What about setting goals and avoiding the common trap of doing everything for other people?

Focusing on number on isn't a selfish thing to do, it's a necessity every now and again. That doesn't mean you should go around focusing all your attention on yourself and not giving a second thought to anyone else, but it does mean placing yourself as a priority every so often and making sure that self-care makes a regular appearance in your routine.

The bottom line is this - if you're pouring all your attention and time into other people, then you're not giving yourself the time or the energy to deal with your own emotions and your own problems. As a result, you're pushing issues to one side and refusing to face them head-on. Over time, these build up and reach a crescendo, which is when difficult emotions start to take over your life and dictate your actions and even your thoughts.

In this chapter, we're going to cover the whole idea of putting yourself first. It's normal to feel a little uncomfortable about doing this because we're always told that we should be selfless and think of others, but there has to be a certain amount of moderation here - you matter too!

You're Stronger When You're Healthier

Self-care is something we should all place as a priority in life. This means doing the things you enjoy, spending time with your own thoughts and checking in on how you're doing every now and again. It's impossible to do this if you're always focusing on other people or in a constant spiral of negativity.

In an earlier chapter, we explored the damaging role of negativity on health and wellbeing, but the same can be said for having the wrong idea about what you should be doing in life. If you're always trying to please other people, focusing on what you should be doing by a certain point in your life, and trying to hit milestones that other people prescribe for you, you're not giving yourself the time and attention you need.

As a result, your mental health suffers, and it's not easy to control negative emotions when you're in a lowered state of mental wellbeing.

For instance, a person who is suffering from anxiety and depression will find it easy to be taken over by their negative emotions, simply because the confidence they need to overcome these thoughts and push forward towards a more positive place isn't present right now. A damaging spiral begins; the emotion takes over, the person reacts in a way they wish they hadn't, they start to beat themselves up about it, and the depression worsens.

This is a spiral that can go on for many years if left unchecked, and there are extremely dire outcomes in this case.

When you're happy and confident, you will find it easier to handle anything which comes your way. That doesn't mean nothing bad is ever going to happen to you or that you're never going to have a down day when you can't think of a nice word to say, but it means you'll be able to keep everything in perspective and recognise it for what it is - a bad day and not a bad life completely.

Confidence is key in life. If you want to get anywhere, you need confidence. If you want to be happy, you need confidence. Heck, confidence can even make you healthier!

Turn your attention inwards and start celebrating your plus points. Recognise the good things you do and celebrate every small milestone along the way. Look for opportunities and make sure you take them if they make sense to where you want to be in life. If the opportunity doesn't present itself, make one for yourself and force life to give you a break. When you're confident, all of this is much easier to do, and when you're lacking in the big C, everything is harder.

It's time to ask yourself what you want from life and start making a plan to go out and get it. When you do this, confidence quickly follows, and the ability to handle any emotion that comes your way.

Why Pleasing Others Means You Don't Please Yourself

The best example of giving, giving, giving, is a parent.

A parent will do anything for their child, often putting themselves so far down the pecking order that they don't get what they need. You might think this is selfless and beautiful, but there comes a time when it can actually become damaging instead.

We've already mentioned that self-care is paramount to overall health and wellbeing, but in terms of being able to manage your emotions, if you don't focus on yourself and feed your body and brain, you're placing yourself in the position to be overtaken by any negativity that comes your way. You might even start to feel a little resentful of the fact that you never get time for yourself, and that in itself might make you feel shameful because you don't think you should be feeling that way.

We're all human, and that means we have needs. Whether you're a parent, a carer, in a relationship, you have a very dependent friendship, or you're simply someone who spends more time giving than receiving, it's normal to want to have time to yourself, it's normal to want to feel loved and to have things come your way for a change. You shouldn't have to spend your entire life giving to other people and pleasing others, it's simply not healthy.

For this reason, making time for yourself is vital.

You can do whatever you want with this time; you can play a sport, go for a run, go for a walk, learn how to paint, sing, learn a language, write a book, read a book, have a bath, you can do whatever you want, as long as it's something you enjoy and find pleasure in. Make it a regular part of your routine, and you'll notice the benefits coming your way.

Of course, pleasing others also has a social aspect to it.

Do you ever feel like you're supposed to reach a certain so-called life milestone by a certain time?

For instance, do you feel pressure to be settled down and married by the time you're 30? Do you feel pressured into having children before the age of 35? Do you worry about the fact that you don't own a house and you're approaching 40?

None of this matters, but we focus on it to the point of debilitating self-esteem issues.

Social milestones are not worth the time or effort. The only milestones you need to focus on are the ones that you want to achieve for yourself, and not for others. If you're constantly living your life trying to hit so-called social norms, you're not focusing on yourself, and you're opening yourself up to all the associated problems we've mentioned so far. As a result, you might also feel angry or resentful of the fact that you're trying to do everything for everyone else, or basically unhappy or as though something is lacking in your life, because you're not doing the things that you want, or you don't actually know what you want.

Do what you want, when you want, and as long as you're not hurting anyone else, they're the only milestones you need to focus on. All of this will make you stronger on the inside and therefore give you a far better chance at dealing with any emotion that comes your way in a healthy and productive manner.

Goal Setting and Emotional Control

With all this talk of doing things for yourself, that leads us seamlessly onto goal setting.

In order to live a happy and fruitful life, you need to set goals.

Sure, you can amble through life and see what opportunities come your way, but you're more likely to get what you want and move in the right direction if you set goals that are personal and important to you.

How does this tie in with emotional control? Because goals give you something to aim for, something to focus on, and something to hold onto when things in life might not be going as you hoped. We all have those times when perhaps a string of bad luck sends us spiralling, but you can choose to either go with it and end up resenting everything, or you can hold firm and stay on track to achieve your goals, come what may.

The second option is a far more positive and healthy outlook to have.

In terms of controlling your emotions, when you have a goal and direction in your life, you're able to put things into perspective and deal with negativity.

You have drive and ambition, and that means you're not going to stop simply because a difficult emotion is trying to make you.

Again, it all loops back toward confidence. When you have confidence, you really do have the power to achieve anything you set your mind to.

So, what goals do you have? Maybe you have some already, or maybe you don't. Either way, it's never too late to start or to get them back on track if they've derailed a little as a result of your emotions getting the better of you.

Any goal you set in life has to be SMART.

That means your goals are :

- **Specific** - You have defined your goal, so you know exactly what you want and how to get it
- **Measurable** - You know how to measure progress, to keep you on track
- **Attainable** - The goal is realistic and not something which you're simply dreaming of
- **Relevant** - The goal takes you towards your greater goals, e.g. your life's aims
- **Time-based** - You have set a timescale in which to achieve your goal

SMART is a term you can apply to any type of goal you set in your life. This can be a personal goal, a goal you need to achieve in order to complete your wok or a dream you have that you want to start working towards.

The key is to break your goals down into manageable pieces, so you're not overloading yourself. When something seems too big, it can become your own personal Everest. That means you're going to procrastinate far easier and end up putting everything off. Have you ever tried to start something in the past and then hit a hurdle and given up? Don't worry if you're nodding your head, everyone has done this at some point in their lives.

What you need to realise, however, is that if you allow these hurdles to constantly derail your goals, you're never going to achieve the things you really want in life. Breaking goals down into smaller, more manageable pieces means that you're making slow yet steady progress towards achieving the end result. Then, when you achieve one milestone, you'll feel full of confidence and motivated to move on to the next one. It's a great way to motivate yourself to keep going when things might seem difficult.

Once you've set your goal and you've checked that every part of it is SMART, you can try another technique to help you along - visualisation.

Remember, all of this has more than one benefit to you. Not only are you moving towards your goals, ticking things off your bucket list, and increasing your confidence, but you're happier as a result. This entire picture is ideal if you want to work towards controlling any negativity that comes into your life and to limit the amount of control negative emotions have on you. When you're focused, and you have an aim such as this, it's far easier to see the bigger picture and realise that having emotional outbursts related to fleeting emotions really isn't worth it.

So, how do you visualise a goal? The aim here is to visualise the goal already being achieved. You need to picture what it looks like, what your life looks like, what it feels like, and every other sensory piece of information you can think of which will tie in with your goal being completed. Visualise the joy you feel and do your best to really tap into it and experience it, feel the pride, and feel the sense of completion. You'll get a small boost of confidence from it all, and it will help you to overcome any obstacles that stand in your way occasionally. There's always one or two, but how you deal with them speaks volumes.

Points to Remember
From This Chapter

This chapter has been about confidence and how you need to focus on yourself occasionally, rather than always trying to please other people.

You might have been a little unsure how this tied into emotional control at the start of the chapter, but by this point, you should be very clear in your mind on how being a confident person with goals, someone who understands the importance of occasional 'me' time, and knows that their needs are just as important as everyone else's, allows you to control your emotions and the reactions that might occur as a result of them.

The main points to take from this chapter are:

- It's perfectly okay to focus your attention on yourself from time to time - it's not selfish, it's necessary
- The expectations of other people don't matter if those expectations aren't in alignment with your own
- You are healthier, stronger, confident and more able to deal with your emotions if you place importance on self-care

- When you're constantly trying to please other people, you're not living your happiest or healthiest life
- Setting goals can give you direction and build your confidence
- Any goals you set need to be SMART, to ensure that you make slow yet steady progress towards their successful completion
- Having goals helps you to control negative emotions because you have an aim in life, and you're more confident as a result.

Chapter 11:

How to Influence Your Emotions And Steer Them in The Right Direction

We've learnt some techniques for helping to control your emotions, but what about in the moment?

Up to this point, we've focused on the bigger picture, e.g. how to create a better foundation so that emotions don't have as much control over you when they rise up and threaten to cause a tsunami. Now, however, we need to look at ways you can deal with a difficult emotion when it hits you.

Life will always throw you curveballs; even if you have a healthier outlook to life and you're ticking every box on your goal list, you're always going to encounter situations throughout your life which challenge your emotions and cause you to feel negative on occasion. This is normal. Whilst you don't always have a choice about what happens in your life, you do have a choice about how you deal with it. That's where your newly discovered emotional control tactics and techniques will come into play.

Remember, emotional control is not something that is going to happen straight away. This is like a muscle that you need to flex and strengthen in order to help it become stronger over time. You can't expect to read this book, try a few techniques and then boom! Everything is solved and you're now a master at dealing with your emotions. It will take time and even when you think you've got a good amount of control, it's normal to experience occasions that threaten to rock your foundations.

Despite that, what you've learnt will stand you in good stead.

Understand That Emotions Are Normal

Before we get on to some practical elements you can use when you're feeling emotional in a specific moment, we need to highlight a very important point.

Up to this section of the book we've talked about emotions and how to deal with them, but that doesn't mean that we should label or stigmatise them as unnatural, bad, or extremely negative. Yes, some emotions are negative, such as anger and jealousy, but we have to feel them because we're human. If you didn't feel these emotions, there would be something quite wrong with you!

Situations come into our lives, as we've just mentioned, and whilst you can't control them, you can control your reaction. That doesn't mean you don't feel the emotion in the first place, and it's important to ensure that you do feel it, that you give yourself the time to actually feel the emotion and how it affects you and your thinking. You can't just ignore emotions because otherwise, you're simply pushing things away.

Feel it. Allow yourself to really feel the way the emotion pushes you, and then choose to react to it in a healthy way, rather than simply allowing the emotion to decide what you're going to do for you. In a way, that's what happens. You're not thinking properly or straight when you're in the middle of a heightened emotion. As a result, you can't make choices because the control has been taken from you. The emotion is holding the reins and deciding what's going to happen.

However, the techniques throughout this book will allow you to take the reins away from the emotion and then steer your actions, words, and thoughts in a direction that is far healthier and productive for you.

Now we've established that fact, and you understand that simply pretending you're not feeling, or pushing emotions away is unhealthy, let's look at 8 ways you can deal with an emotional moment when you're actually in the middle of it.

8 Ways You Can Influence And Control Your Emotions

These methods are very useful to use when you're noticing your emotions rising, or when they've already risen, and you're feeling like you're about to blow. This emotion can be anything, from anger to jealousy, shame to despair, basically anything which is a threat to how you act and control yourself at the moment you're in.

You might find all of these methods useful, or you might simply find that a few work for you. The number doesn't matter, all that matters is that you're working towards finding a 'go-to' method that you can use and you know is successful in your situation.

As you're learning how to handle your emotions, it's important that you also begin to notice your own personal signs. This means when you can tell an emotion is coming your way. It's like a slow build that suddenly bursts; so, how can you recognise the emotion before it gets to bursting point? By being more aware of yourself and how you feel in the moment.

Do you remember a little earlier in the book we talked about mindfulness?

Mindfulness helps you to stay in the moment you're in, i.e. the present day and stops you from living in the past or jumping to the future. Mindfulness will also help you to be aware of how you're feeling from moment to moment. By doing this, you can recognise a building emotion before it gets to a point where you have to step in with some damage limitation.

Everyone has a different type of feeling when they're about to experience an emotional high; you might feel anxious, perhaps you notice physical symptoms such as suddenly feeling hot or starting to shake, or maybe you just have a 'sinking' feeling in the pit of your stomach. You'll come to realise your own personal signs as you become more mindful of how you feel from moment to moment.

Once you've become familiar with those signs, you can effectively use the techniques we're going to talk about below.

1 - Question Whether You're Dealing With a Trigger

When you notice an emotion coming your way, stop and ask yourself whether you're dealing with a trigger. Of course, this hinges on you knowing your own triggers in the first place. A little earlier in the book, we talked about emotion journals, and this is one of the single best ways to really look into what causes your emotions to ebb and flow.

Once you've identified a trigger, you can easily question whether or not you're about to encounter one, or whether the signs you're experiencing are as a result of being close to a personal trigger.

When you confirm that you are indeed dealing with one of your own personal emotional triggers, the situation eases because you can tell yourself that the trigger doesn't hold control over you. Tell yourself that you are on the one with the reins in your hand, that your trigger is unimportant and simply a thing or an issue which is trying to wrestle the reins of control from your hands. Do not let it win.

You might like to visualise yourself holding the reins in your hands, holding them tight and not letting anything take them away from you. By doing this, you're taking yourself away from the emotion for a second and distracting your mind. Much of the time, that is enough to let the peak of the emotion pass, and you can then start to work on taking your mind away from any adverse reaction that might occur.

2 - Take Yourself Away From The Situation For a Moment

The best way to calm down when you're noticing a rising emotion is to take yourself away from the situation for a second and work on calming yourself down. Nine times out of ten, this will stop you from reacting adversely without thinking. Of course, you might still react, but at least you'll react in a more informed way.

You can walk away from the situation when you know there's a trigger in front of you, or you can continue until you feel like you're getting to a point where your emotions are getting the better of you. When that happens, recognise your tipping point and take yourself away from the room. If you can, go outside into the fresh air, because that will allow you to refocus and calm down far easier and quicker. If you can't go outside, simply go anywhere that isn't near the trigger or the situation that's causing the problem.

Once you're away, make sure you're alone and focus on something still. This can be the wall, a tree, the grass, anything on the wall that isn't moving. Then, when you're ready, turn your attention towards your breath and use the deep breathing exercises we mentioned in our earlier chapter.

After a short while, you will notice that you're far calmer and you've adverted a negative reaction as a result. Only go back into the situation when you're ready, and you feel like you've side-stepped a major issue. Then, continue to focus on your breathing by simply observing it. This will keep you calm and stop your emotions rising for a second time.

3 - Ask Yourself Whether Your Feelings Are Proportionate

When you notice that your emotions are starting to rise, stop for a second, take yourself off to the side and analyse yourself for a moment. Ask yourself "why do I feel this way?" Dig a little deeper and question whether your reaction and the way you feel is actually proportionate to what is going on around you to cause the emotion to rise.

The chances are, once you start to pull things apart for just a few seconds, you'll see that there is no reason for an adverse reaction. By doing this, you give yourself just enough time to see sense, to know that if you continue and allow yourself to get to the point where your control is diminished, the damage will be worse than the situation you're in now.

Again, mindfulness is ideal for keeping things in proportion. We tend to panic when we're noticing a heightened emotion, and a lot of that is about feeling helpless or out of control. Taking steps to analyse that emotion and realising that it's nowhere near as powerful as you're allowing it to be, you'll be able to handle the situation better in the moment and avert an issue.

4 - Look For a Positive

The ideal distraction technique is to quickly notice that you're feeling an emotion rising up and then look for a position. Look around you and look quickly. What is there around your or within you that is positive and which you're thankful for? This can quickly turn your emotional state from negative to positive, because you're literally taking a hammer and hitting negativity on the head!

The positive thing you look for can be anything. It can be the sun in the sky, the fact that you're wearing your favourite outfit that day, you've got a date later on, or you're about to eat your favourite food. Find a positive and focus on it intensely. After a few minutes, you'll start to calm down, and you'll be able to deal with the emotion in a calmer and more retrospective kind of way.

5 - Give The Emotion a Name

Another very effective way to deal with emotions is to give them a name. Labelling something means that it's a thing, and we all know that we can deal with 'things'. By naming an emotion you can also quickly see whether it is positive or negative, and if it's negative, you have a head's up that you need to avert disaster and give yourself a few minutes away from the situation.

Again, in order to do this, you need to be able to recognise how certain emotions feel to you, but this shouldn't be too difficult. When you feel something, name it, so say "I am feeling angry", "I am feeling jealous", "I feel ashamed", or "I feel anxious and worried".

Dealing with the unknown is scary, but dealing with something you're aware of isn't.

6 - Reframe Your Thoughts, Not Just The Negative

In our chapter on becoming more positive, we talked about a technique called 'reframing'. Reframing can be used in a variety of different situations and whilst it's very useful in changing your mindset and becoming more positive, it can be used when dealing with an emotion in the moment too. In this case, you're not reframing your attitude from negative to positive, but you're reframing your thoughts and the way you see the situation that is causing your emotions to rise.

For example, perhaps someone in your work is your own personal emotional trigger. This person often causes you to feel angry because they come over as rude and stand-offish and you don't feel like they give you the respect you deserve. They might have said something flippant or dismissed you, and as a result, you're starting to feel angry. Rather than allowing that thought to lead you down towards an anger response, take yourself away for a second and think about it.

Take the thought you're having, e.g. 'I don't like this person, they're always rude and dismissive' and then dig a little deeper. Perhaps this person is dealing with something at home that is causing them to act in a certain way. Perhaps this person is a little shy and that shyness comes over as rudeness without them meaning it to be. Find an alternative thought that is more positive than the first one, and focus on it.

As a result, you might be able to understand the situation through different eyes, but you might also notice that your emotions around that situation aren't as heightened as before.

There is always more than one way to look at something and it could very well be that you really have got the 'wrong end of the stick'!

7 - Do Something You Enjoy

Moving on from the earlier point we made about taking yourself away from the situation to calm down, if the emotion you're feeling isn't going to cause an explosion, e.g. anger, you could instead take yourself away and do something you enjoy.

Much of the time, when you distract your mind with fun things, or things which bring you personal joy, the emotion you were experiencing simply disappears without you even noticing it. As a result, it holds far less power over you and you're able to deal with it in a healthier way than otherwise.

So, if you're noticing that you're struggling with a particular emotion, pick up the phone and call a friend for a gossiping session, head out to your favourite coffee shop and treat yourself to coffee and take, go for a run and pound the pavements, or go to the cinema and watch that film you've been meaning to see. Distraction isn't always about not dealing with a situation, sometimes it's simply about averting an emotional response that isn't helpful or necessary.

8 - Understand That Practice Makes Perfect

Some of the time when you try and control the way you're feeling in the moment, you might not do the best job. That's fine, understand that practice really does make perfect in this case. This particular point might not be a technique you can do, but it's something to remember when you're struggling.

Provided you're making positive steps towards trying to control your emotions and live a life which isn't so heavily dictated by the way you're feeling, you're already the one in control. The reason? Because you're working towards a situation that is far more positive, and you have to understand that in order to do that, you need to practice.

Look back at some of the times when you tried to control your emotions and succeeded. Take heart with every single time that happens and if one time it doesn't work, just shrug it off and try again the next time. The more you do it, the abler you'll become.

Forgive yourself for the times your emotional control efforts didn't work and tell yourself "I'm doing my best".

Points to Remember
From This Chapter

This chapter has covered how you can deal with an emotional response when it is happening, mostly by recognising what is happening and taking steps to avoid disaster. The strategies contained within this chapter should help you to avoid any potential fallout before it occurs. It's far better to avoid trouble than deal with it after the event!

Despite that, it's also important to realise that trying to avoid feeling an emotion isn't healthy either. We have emotions for a reason and it's part and parcel of life to have ups and downs. However, you always have a choice in terms of how you react to it, and that's where you need to aim your efforts.

Realise that emotions are normal, but that you're the one in control of your actions.

The main points to take from this chapter are:

- Emotions are a normal part of being human
- It's not healthy to try not to feel your emotions, because they're trying to teach you something. Feel them, but understand that the control is in your hands
- Learn to know your own emotional signs, so you can identify when you're starting to feel

particularly emotional. This might include shaking, feeling unsure, or perhaps a 'sinking' feeling. Once you know your signs, you can work to divert disaster

- Taking yourself away from a situation which is causing you to feel a negative emotion is a good starting point, and from there you can unpick the situation or try and alleviate it, before returning and feeling calmer as a result
- You may find that your efforts don't work all the time at first, and even as you become more experienced at handling and dealing with your emotions, there may be times when you're simply not successful. That's fine. You just have to carry on practising and tell yourself that you're doing your very best.

Chapter 12:
The Art of Stress Management

How do you feel about your efforts to control your emotions now?

We're nearing the end fo the book, and the hope is that you're feeling upbeat and positive about your chances of taking back control of the reins and learning to live a happier and more positive life as a result.

We've talked a lot about health and wellbeing so far, and we've given you many tactics to actually handle emotions and control your reactions, but there is one enemy which might derail your efforts completely - stress.

Stress is on the rise.

We live in a time that is constantly connected, constantly demanding and often full of negativity. We've already talked about how to reduce negativity, but stress could still derail everything, due to its extreme force.

Stress can come from a variety of different elements of life. You can feel stressed in your personal life, perhaps from your relationship, your lack of a relationship, friendships or family issues. You might feel stressed due to money problems, or you might be experiencing workplace stress, which is certainly one of the most common. Stress can also occur as a result of an event, perhaps moving house, getting married, illness, or something else entirely.

Put simply, whatever is stressing you out is your own personal stressor, but that doesn't mean that it's less important than anyone else's.

What you need to realise is that stress is dangerous. How many times per day do you hear someone saying "oh I'm so stressed", when in reality they're just a little bit busy and have a few more jobs to do that day? Stress, in reality, is something far more serious and not something which should be put down or less importance placed upon it.

In this chapter, we're going to explore stress and its role in how you control and handle your emotions. We're also going to give you some useful stress management tips you can try. You might also be surprised to learn that many stress management techniques overlap with regular emotional control techniques too!

Why Stress is Dangerous For Health And Wellbeing

Stress can be a silent killer. Yes, stress can be fatal.

Think about that for a second and assess how you feel about it.

By suffering from stress, you're actually putting your health and wellbeing at risk in a big, big way. This affects every single part of your life too; your relationships suffer, your work suffers, your productivity in general suffers, your focus suffers, and you might make mistakes that are uncharacteristic. Stress can also cause you to enter into unhealthy situations which could affect your emotions directly, such as developing unhealthy coping mechanisms for dealing with the stressor itself.

We've already talked about the stress response, i.e. the fight or flight response, but we haven't mentioned that during that response, many different hormones are released into the bloodstream. Of course, this is necessary to help you deal with a potential problem or threat that your mind perceives to be dangerous, but most of the time there isn't a direct threat to your health or your survival, it's a threat to your day.

172

For instance, you might feel stressed about a work deadline. The stress response will start because you start to feel panicky about not meeting the deadline. Your brain recognises that and thinks 'wait for a second, there's a threat here', and it floods the body with all the necessary things it needs to survive that threat. That means cortisol (stress hormone) is increased, as well as adrenaline and other chemicals.

If there was a real threat, e.g. a very large animal was coming after you and was going to eat you, those chemicals and hormones would be very useful. They would give you the energy and the supplements in your legs to run away very fast and hide somewhere until the threat passed. However, it's not that kind of threat.

As a result, these chemicals and hormones are in your system without a reason, and when that happens, they tend to stick around longer than they should. Extra stress is therefore placed upon your heart, your respiratory system, your body might tense up, causing aches and pains, and your immune system starts to take a battering over the long-term too.

Put simply, you're living in a constant state of stress, a heightened sense of awareness, and it's just not healthy for your physical or your mental health.

Over time this can worsen, and the impact on your bodily organs and your mental health can lead to conditions that may end up being fatal in the long term.

So, the next time someone tells you that they're "so stressed", think for a second about whether they really are!

How Stress Affects Your Emotions

How does this all tie into your emotions?

When you're in a state of stress, i.e. you're in the middle of the fight or flight stress response, it's very easy to become overly emotional. It's hard to control anything because your body is constantly aware of every single thing and trying to work out whether it's a threat to your survival or not. This means you're not in the best state of mind, your anxiety is heightened, you're worrying, overthinking, and you're not feeling very healthy on the inside.

It's a very poor foundation on which to build emotional control.

When you're feeling stressed, you're far more likely to feel anxious or fearful, you might be moody or irritable, and depression is far more likely. We've already talked about the fact that when you're feeling negative in terms of your emotions, what is going on inside your brain is affected too. Your brain chemistry is altered, and this can also lead you towards a greater risk of stress.

As you can see, it's a pretty dangerous cycle that will simply keep going around and around.

Stress, in general, is likely to make you feel more negative, and we've already talked about dangerous that can be!

The Symptoms of Stress

You might not even realise that you're stressed! Many people who have been living in a state of stress for a long time don't actually realise it. They feel like everything is a little too much or that they're unhealthy or negative, but they don't realise that at the heart of it is the fact that they're in the middle of a stress response that's been stuck on "on" for too long.

It's important to recognise the symptoms of stress, both physically and mentally, so you can work to reduce the issue in your life.

The problem is, stress can affect people in many different ways, and that means looking at things from a personal point of view. Stress symptoms can be categorised into three groups - physical, psychological/cognitive, and emotional.

The main symptoms of stress are:

Emotional Symptoms

- Very easily agitated with those around you
- A sense of being overwhelmed
- Not being able to switch off or relax
- Low self-esteem
- Self-imposed isolation, e.g. staying away from people and wanting to be alone

Psychological/Cognitive Symptoms

- Anxiety and a constant state of being worried
- Overthinking
- Being forgetful
- Not being able to concentrate or focus
- Making bad decisions on a regular basis
- Having a negative mind-set

Physical Symptoms

- Lacking in energy
- Regular headaches
- Stomach problems, such as feeling sick, constipation or diarrhoea
- Feeling achy generally
- A fast heartbeat
- Not being able to sleep well, or at all
- Regularly picking up viruses and colds
- Grinding teeth or clenching jaw without being aware of it
- A dry mouth
- Feeling nervous or shaky for no reason
- Sweating
- Loss of libido

Of course, we have to exercise a certain amount of caution when deciding whether or not you're stressed from this list of symptoms alone, because many of them can be down to another problem. For instance, a racing heartbeat should be checked out by your doctor, especially if it's associated with chest pain. Similarly, you should get regular headaches checked out too.

However, if you can agree on several of the symptoms on that list, the chances are that you're suffering from chronic stress. In that case, you need to work towards minimising the stress in your life, therefore improving your health and wellbeing, improving your mood, and also helping you gain better control over your emotions and emotional reactions.

10 Effective Stress Management Techniques

In this section, we're going to cover 10 techniques which can help you to effectively manage stress, and therefore improve your emotional control almost as a side effect. As we've already mentioned, many of the techniques used for stress management are mirrored in emotional control anyway.

1. **Do your best to have a positive attitude as much as possible** - when you're stressed, everything is dragged down to the negative. Use reframing, mindfulness, positive affirmations and visualisation techniques to help you develop a more positive and healthier mind-set.

2. **Realise that life isn't all about control** - Whilst we're trying to control our emotions in this book, it's important to realise that you can't control everything else in life. Things will happen, good and bad, and that whilst most of those events can't be controlled, you can grab back the reins by controlling your reaction. You don't have to allow yourself to become stressed, and you don't have to react in an emotional way. Understanding this is a great stepping stone towards managing stress.

3. **Talk about the problem** - What is it that is causing you to feel stressed? Spend some time really thinking about it and coming to a

conclusion. Then, find someone you trust and who you can really sit and talk to, and get everything out. Talking about a stressor can actually reduce its strength because when you talk about something, you often see how weak or ridiculous it really is! Talking to someone also gives you the benefit of their advice and insight. Perhaps you're making a mountain out of a molehill, and your friend can help you to see that and banish the stressor.

4. **Focus on your health and wellbeing** - Just as you can't control your emotions on an unhealthy foundation, you can't banish stress on an unhealthy foundation either. Focus on your health and wellbeing. Make sure you're eating a healthy diet, packed with vitamins and minerals and that you're cutting down on foods that can actually exacerbate stress, such as processed foods, too much red meat, caffeine and sugar-laden drinks. You can handle stress far better when you're feeling healthy on the inside.

5. **Exercise regularly** - Exercise is one of the best ways to manage stress because it releases feel-good endorphins and also gives you a break from your mind. When you're exercising, you're probably distracted from the problem at hand. When you don't think about something for a short while, even just 10 minutes, it's often less powerful when it comes back into your mind; it can't be that important if you forgot about it for a short while! Exercise also keeps your body and

mind fit, which allows you to deal with stress in a far more positive and productive way.

6. **Try different relaxation techniques** - We've already covered several deep breathing techniques that can be used for stress relief and relaxation, but what about trying other relaxation methods such as yoga, pilates, or perhaps meditation? If all that fails, simply taking a hot bath and reading a book you enjoy can be just as relaxing!

7. **Learn to manage your time** - Sometimes we become stressed because we can't organise our time. This means that we're always chasing our tails and feeling overwhelmed. Take back control of your time by creating a to-do list and prioritising it in order importance or urgency. By doing this, you're making small steps towards getting done everything you need to, and you'll feel more upbeat and confident as a result.

8. **Learn that it's okay to say "no" sometimes** - In our chapter on looking after yourself we mentioned that you can't always please other people, and within that, you need to learn to say "no" occasionally. If you're snowed under with work, don't feel like you have to agree to something you really don't have the time to do. If you don't want to do something, sometimes it's fine to refuse in a polite way. Make time for yourself and do things you enjoy; that can be

reading a book, going shopping, watching a film, or simply doing nothing!

9. **Focus on sleep** - Just as you should focus on exercise and health, you cannot be free of stress if you're not rested. Make sure you're getting at least 7 to 8 hours of sleep every night and make sure that you have a regular sleeping routine. By doing that, you'll be well-rested and have more energy, allowing you to deal with stressors more effectively, banish negativity and generally be healthier overall.

10. **Spend time with people who make you feel good** - It's very easy to hide away when you're feeling stressed, because you just don't want to talk about things, but that's actually a very counterproductive thing to do. Instead, make sure you spend at least some time with other people and try and spend more time with those who make you feel uplifted. If someone regularly makes you laugh, ask them if they want to go out for a coffee and enjoy a few hours in their company! By the end, you're sure to feel better, and the social element will help you to overcome the stress you're feeling.

As you can see, there is no rocket science in dealing with stress, it's simply about focusing on the important things and realising that you can only do so much.

We all try and do too much, simply because we have no rest period. We're always connected via the Internet or other means, so it's easy for other people to ask a favour, or for your manager to give you another task to do. As a result, you're never free to simply just 'be'. There is a lot to be said for just 'being'!

Of course, if you feel like stress is starting to cause you detrimental effects, perhaps if you feel unwell or you feel like you can't cope, then you should seek out medical help. Your doctor will be more than happy to sit down and talk to you about how you're feeling and the experiences you're going through, both in terms of your symptoms and the things in your life which you feel could be having an effect on your stress levels.

From there, there are many different treatment and therapy methods you can use, including counselling. Never be afraid to reach out for help. Far too many people worry about the stigma attached to saying "help me", but it's actually the strongest thing you can do in life. Once you admit that you might need a bit of support, the wheels of healing and recovery can begin. From there, you'll notice that your health and wellbeing improve, your stress levels reduce, and your ability to control your emotions is far greater too.

Points to Remember
From This Chapter

This chapter has been a bumper one! We've talked in detail about stress and how it is dangerous for your health and wellbeing, whilst damaging your ability to control your emotions in the moment and the reactions you have afterwards.

Remember, if you feel you are struggling, be sure to reach out for help and advice. There is no shame in it, and you'll be putting yourself on the road to recovery as a result. We've also talked about some useful stress management techniques you can try, and all of them are ideal methods to incorporate into your life, as they'll help you deal with a variety of different situations, whilst also making you healthier as a result.

The main points to take from this chapter are:

- Stress is dangerous and should never be underestimated
- Stress can be fatal in the worst-case scenarios
- When you're stressed, it's almost impossible to be able to control your emotions
- Stress is personal and can cover a range of severities and be for a range of reasons
- Reaching out for help with stress is not a failing, but a strength

- There are many different stress management techniques you can try, and many of them will make you healthier and allow you to deal with your emotions more productively at the same time.

Conclusion

And there we have it!

You've reached the end of the book, and by now you should be feeling full of energy and inspiration to help in your own emotional control efforts.

Remember, there is no shame in admitting that perhaps your emotions have more control over you than you do over them. There is, however, shame in simply allowing the situation to continue in that way for the rest of your life, and not doing anything to change it.

We've talked about the fact that a lack of emotional control can play havoc in your life, and it can also lead you to low self-esteem and poor mental health. If you're constantly at the mercy of your emotions, you're probably not going to get as much done as you wanted to, which will lead to stress, and as a result, you're going to put yourself into a very unhealthy situation.

You might also damage relationships in your life, simply because your emotional outbursts or your worries about what may or may not be happening might take over.

Being able to appreciate the fact that emotions happen is part and parcel of learning to control them. You can't stop them from happening, but you can choose how you react to them. The emotions themselves are part of being human – if you didn't feel them, you wouldn't be human!

As you work through the chapters in this book, try all the techniques we mention but remember that not all may work for you. We're all individual, and that might mean that some are more effective than others. After you've identified the useful techniques for you personally, work on those more intensely, and use them in a way that suits you best.

Every self-development journey in life is about focusing on yourself and what you need to be able to improve and develop the areas of your life which need attention. By understanding that perhaps you need to help in controlling your emotions, you've taken the first step. That acknowledgement is all you need to set light a fire under your intentions and start making positive steps. However, you shouldn't expect miracles overnight!

Work slowly, methodically and celebrate every success you have along the way.

What if You Can't Control an Emotion?

Before we bid you goodbye, we should give a quick acknowledgement to the fact that sometimes emotional control fails. Even the most Zen person out there is going to have an off day! Don't beat yourself up if this happens, it's normal, but it shouldn't be a regular occurrence and should be a very occasional and very rare deal.

If this happens, first acknowledge it and give yourself time to recover. Forgive yourself and realise that you've had a set-back, but you can get back on track. Then, give yourself some space and time to sit down and really think back over what you could have done differently. By doing this, you can learn lessons for next time, and then you'll be able to sidestep the same issue that has caused you a problem this time.

Most of the time, that simply means apologising for anyone you had an outburst towards, and realising that you need to focus on a new or strengthened trigger.

It's possible that you will develop new triggers as you go through your life. You can combat a list of triggers that you already have right now, but you need to always be on the lookout for possible new situations in your life which might have an effect on your emotions. However, these should become less and less, as you learn to be more positive and more able to see the bigger picture.

As you learn to control your emotions, you will become more confident in yourself. This is going to lead you towards new opportunities, some you'll take and some you won't. The ones you do take may change the course of your life, but will also lead you into situations you might not have dealt with before. For many people, the unknown and change can be a trigger, and that is something which you may never be able to overcome completely. However, learning to see these opportunities as fun events, things you can see as an adventure, and a challenge is a good way to start.

With that, it's time to bid you goodbye.

I wish you luck in your emotional control journey and know that with the advice we've given you throughout this book, you have every chance of success. All it takes is a little perseverance, effort, time, and focus. If you can put forth those elements, there will be no stopping you.

Good luck!

A Short message from the Author:

Hey, are you enjoying the book? I'd love to hear your thoughts!

Many readers do not know how hard reviews are to come by, and how much they help an author. It is generally reviews alone that can persuade another person to choose this book.

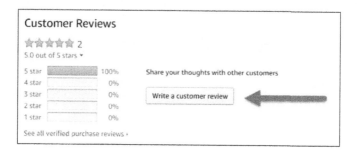

60 seconds is all it takes to write a brief review – even if it's just a few sentences – on Amazon, Audible, Goodreads, or whatever bookstore you purchased this book from!

Thank you for taking the time to share your thoughts!

<u>More from Jean-Claude Leveque</u>

-Conquer your Motivation

-Conquer your Concentration

-Conquer your Purpose

-F*ck Anxiety

-F*ck Panic Attacks

Made in the USA
Monee, IL
23 July 2023

39751334R00114